FIGHTING FOR CONTROL

Kirsty Vincent

DEDICATION

To my family, for your love and your blessing in the
creation of this book.

To my friends, for your unwavering support.

To my colleagues, for your enduring patience and
kindness.

And to my readers, may you find reassurance within
these pages that you are not alone.

INTRODUCTION

A friend suggested I should write this book. I consider myself incredibly fortunate: I have survived a diagnosis of Post-Traumatic Stress Disorder and have managed to fight my way through hell. I've made enough progress through therapy to now be back working in my chosen career, in the fire service control room. I am also in the privileged position of being able to share my experiences where others cannot. I know full well that some people can't get to where I am today; they can't speak of their trauma or stop it from haunting them day to day. Some people, devastatingly, lose their lives to it; others may survive but lose friends, family, their home, their job. They lose themselves. So, my goal is to try to do what I can to help those who suffer, particularly emergency service workers for whom I feel PTSD still isn't noticed or acknowledged enough. Writing this is my way of raising awareness, underlining symptoms, and explaining how to recognise signs of PTSD in others and therefore assist in how to support them.

This introduction is also a plea to all my readers: please understand that my writing is a reflection of the state of mind I was in throughout this whole journey. I apologise if it reads a little harshly in places. I was a mess and very broken, and this was my perspective at the time. But I need this book to stay true and honestly raw – otherwise I don't feel that other people who are struggling will identify with my words. I hate the fact that loved ones may have got caught in the crossfire of my sometimes brutal opinions. All the individuals mentioned within this book – those I still see in my day-to-day life, those I work with or love – please know that whatever you may read in these pages is not meant to hurt or insult you. Instead, it's intended to represent how I perceived things at the time. I took everything so personally, and my sensitive state of mind felt wounded by the slightest of interactions, where normally I wouldn't have been affected. It didn't take a lot to make me spiral – wrong words, misguided actions – but including them in this book is meant to show how vulnerable PTSD can make someone who is normally so confident and sure of both themselves and their support networks. It's a reminder for those struggling that you're not alone, and a confirmation for those in supporting positions that your actions are appreciated, even if not always received how they were meant!

Every person involved in this journey has had their name changed to ensure anonymity to the wider public. You all know who you are, and despite my mood swings, misunderstandings or grievances, I know you are the best group of people, who have dragged me back to living my life again. Thank you so much.

This is my story.

CHAPTER 1
EARLY YEARS

I remember having an incredibly happy childhood, with a stable home life, and I probably had a rose-tinted view of the world. I'm grateful that nothing traumatic really happened to me growing up. Looking back, I consider myself to have been an upbeat, emotional, but resilient child. Daring and always willing to try new things, I threw myself into fresh opportunities whenever they presented themselves. New club at school? I'd sign up. Big rollercoaster? I'd try it. Abseiling on a residential trip? I was one of the first down that waterfall. I'd learnt from an early age to give anything a go once: on a trip with the Brownies, when I was about seven or eight, we'd had an evening booked to use the local climbing wall. I was scared to attempt the difficult level, which had fewer footholds and scaled higher than the easier section. So I ended up not trying it. By the end of the evening, I was kicking myself, furious to have missed my chance and regretting my decision to dip out just because of fear. Since that day, I've always pushed myself to do things even when I'm scared; at least then I can say I've given it a go, and not feel regret afterwards.

I was known by my family to wear my heart on my sleeve, certainly in my younger years. I'd have "happy tears" and stroppy moments too. I'm the eldest of three, with parents who are still happily married, and who continue, to this day, to live in the house where I grew up.

I remember a particular moment, when I must have been nine or ten years old, that was a huge learning point for me. It taught me the need to control my feelings at appropriate times. This lesson was to become highly relevant in the years to come.

My dad had chosen to take us all to watch stock car racing. It was very exciting. I remember my brother, the middle child, being terrified of the noise, while my younger sister, five years my junior, took it all in. As we drove home after a long day, on a fast, 60mph road, a man stepped out of the bushes and hit my parents' car. It transpired that he was intoxicated. He'd been drinking all day at a wedding and was now trying to walk home along a busy B-road. I was sitting in the nearside rear seat and I saw the whole thing. I completely freaked out. I was convinced my dad had driven into and killed the man; was sure he'd end up going to prison on the back of it.

My dad obviously stopped the car and investigated. As it turned out, the man's hand had clipped the car's wing mirror, causing the mirror to fold back with a bang, but he was otherwise unharmed. I was then paranoid that this scary stranger was going to attack my father; that he might have weapons on him. I totally panicked, and my dad, who was a strict but loving and kind father, rather sharply told me to shut up and stop screaming. In hindsight, he was probably panicking too, and my hysterical response added stress he didn't need. I did shut up, shocked into silence that he'd raised his voice like that to me. I also realised my bad reaction was worrying my siblings.

The situation resolved itself. My dad called the police, who responded promptly to take custody of the drunken wedding guest. We then continued our journey home. But I learnt a lot that day and I remember the moment vividly: panicking and screaming in a pressured or emergency situation does nothing but worsen the circumstances and panic everyone around you. And in fact, it is possible to swallow those scared feelings and deal with the matter in hand.

More life lessons landed as I turned eighteen years old. I'll keep the details vague as I don't feel my family would appreciate their lives being laid out here, but I think these events are all-important to my story and need to be mentioned. My amazing mum sustained an injury at work. The injury developed into a rare medical condition that eventually led to her becoming permanently disabled. This had various wide-reaching effects. Her whole being understandably changed to cope with her new reality. She became much more emotional, anxious and withdrawn, and she suffered a lot of pain. My dad tried to gain a sense of control over the situation but was clearly stressed and found it hard to deal with. At around this time, he was also trying to handle the passing of both his parents, my grandparents, within a few years of each other. My sister, the youngest of the three of us and just into her early teens, took the accident particularly hard. She became incredibly protective of my mum, often insisting she would do things to help her that she felt we were unable to do "properly". As my mum's condition gradually worsened, my sister's need to take on the role of carer grew more intense. She had a mental health blip herself in her later teens, which I believe was partly attributable to this.

My sister having a tough time was difficult; she made some bad decisions. My parents blamed themselves for her actions and excused her from it all. In my eyes, she was then treated with kid gloves for years afterwards, spoilt through a sense of guilt. My parents refused to let us talk about it; they didn't want us to fall out and tried to avoid rows between us by burying the situation. The consequence of this was a build-up of anger and resentment on my part. My sister made some decisions that left me fuming and yet I wasn't allowed to voice anything. Mum and Dad loved us all dearly, still do, and just wanted to keep the peace with everyone. My brother is very mellow and kept out of any drama; he silently offered support to my mum, and I'd say he is the closest to her out of the three of us. He also became more of a buddy to my sister, particularly when I moved out of the family home in the years to come.

Through all of this, I learnt several things: first, that my parents, despite their best intentions, didn't know how to approach mental health issues. My mum's struggles in coming to terms with her illness, my dad trying to cope and my sister's situation were all ignored, buried or glossed over. They weren't addressed. Mental illness was still seen as a sort of taboo in our family – things happened, and you carried on. Secondly, I learnt that life is short. You have no idea when things might change quickly, so you should live every day to the full, in case one day you can't. Thirdly, time can heal certain things but talking is so important. I held a grudge and a lot of resentment towards my sister, which didn't help either of us over the years. Things are a lot better now, but it's taken a fair while to get to that place.

I've always worked for the fire service in one way or another. My interest began when I joined a fire cadet scheme at the age of fourteen. I was able to secure two lots of work experience through my station and was lucky enough to follow the watches for a week on station in my last year of school. I then got involved in the Community Safety department when I was in sixth form a year later. Teenage-me knew this was what I wanted to do – it seemed exciting and rewarding, and my goal at the time was to become a wholetime firefighter.

The Community Safety department seemed to like me and I was hired on a casual basis shortly afterwards as an instructor, working for a programme called "Junior Citizens". This was a whole safety scheme set up to educate ten- to eleven-year-olds in various interactive situations. I absolutely loved it and felt I gained a rapport with the kids I taught. The scheme only ran for certain weeks of the year, so it was perfect to slot around my sixth-form studies. I still instruct JCs now and am in my fourteenth year of doing so.

One of the benefits of working in the Community Safety department was that I got to talk to lots of staff members of various agencies, including firefighters, control staff, police officers and healthcare workers. They all advised the same: to get the job I was after, I needed life experience.

Once my studies ended, I had several part-time jobs on the go. I continued with JCs and became an instructor for two fire cadet units too; I worked in an office and I juggled a retail job at a home store alongside it. I thrived on the variety of each day but I realised retail work wasn't for me long term. The office position was mundane data processing and was a temporary position. I knew I wanted to try something completely different and that I seemed to have a skill in instructing children. So, I applied to become an instructor at an activity centre that had set-ups around the country. I was fortunate enough to be accepted and, after two weeks of training in Kent, I relocated to my chosen centre on the Isle of Wight.

I spent six months in a summer season working on the island; long, twelve-hour days on a next-to-nothing apprentice wage – and I loved every second of it. We all lived in a shared house in a beautiful village five minutes' walk from the beach. At the age of twenty, it was my first taste of independence. I met some amazing people and made the most of my days off too – the Isle of Wight is stunning and I was very pleased to have my car to explore the length of it. Even today, the island is a familiar home-from-home to me, always a calming retreat when I just need a breather.

As the summer season ended, I received a message from an old cadet colleague and friend, who happened to be the watch manager for the retained – also known as on-call – crew at my hometown fire station. They were shortly to run a recruitment campaign for on-call personnel and he wanted to know if I'd be interested. I applied, moved back to the family home, and tackled each stage of the process while picking up JCs and instructing cadets again in the meantime. I was successful and over the moon. I started training, and collected my alerter to be on call one week before my twenty-first birthday.

CHAPTER 2
RETAINED

I had a good idea what to expect from my new role, having spent years involved with fire stations. It had prepared me to an extent for the years to come: I enjoyed the banter and dark humour of firefighters, and I had an understanding of why it took a particular personality to fulfil this role. Nevertheless, my first day on call was one I would never forget.

My alerter went off. I responded to the station, full of adrenaline, to be told we'd been stood down. I was disappointed but went home. It went off a second time, for us to make it two roads away from the station, before the same thing happened.

Evening came and the beeper sounded for a third time that day. This time, it was a job: reports of a road traffic collision (RTC) and potential fatalities. I jumped on the pump and off we went to a country road about five minutes out of town. My crew manager in charge of the incident was very good and kept an eye on me. He was aware that my first ever shout was likely to be a nasty one. He also told me that no one really knows how they'll react to their first dead body – but it was important to remain professional in the public eye.

We booked in attendance with Control and it was clear the driver of the vehicle was deceased. He'd been driving the van round a bend in the road, had lost control and the vehicle had hit a tree. The driver's neck was broken on impact. My crew manager gave me the choice to get close to the body or to limit my exposure: I chose the former. I had a morbid curiosity over wanting to know how I'd manage, and I found I could cope well. What I'd discovered at the age of ten was now being put to good use – it was possible to compartmentalise what I was feeling and get on with the job in hand.

I was given the task of searching the nearby fields with a colleague and a Thermal Imaging Camera. This was to check that no passengers had been involved in the crash and fled the wreck. To my relief, the TIC picked up nothing. We came away from that incident fairly quickly once the scene was made safe. My crew manager checked in with me to make sure I was all right, we returned to the station and I drove home.

On my arrival there, my parents made a joke about me attending station only to be stood down on shouts. I remember shutting them down and being quite short with them in general that evening as I tried to process events. After being told I was being rude and bad-tempered, I retaliated with the information that I'd just returned from a fatality RTC. That completely changed the mood of the room: there was an unsure reaction and a lot of sympathy.

I didn't want sympathy. Nor, I realised, could I talk about it with them: from their hesitant, almost scared response, I realised I'd never be able to talk about my work to my family. I love them to bits, but that one incident created in my mind a divide I couldn't ignore. They'd never understand as they'd never experienced similar events. I didn't want to worry them, and I couldn't deal with their sympathy and their shock.

So it was that my colleagues – both at station and particularly at JCs – became my confidants if jobs were tough, and I found myself maintaining that emotional distance from my family and my "civilian" friends. I seemed to attract the nasty incidents and I was getting a bit of a reputation because of it. In quick succession after my first call, there followed a fatal house fire and then a drowning in the local reservoir.

My station was a two-pump, wholetime and retained station within a fairly big town on the edge of a motorway, surrounded by villages. This meant I was exposed to a lot of varied situations. Despite the occasional traumatic sight, I loved my new job and felt I was making a difference in the local community. I attended a thatch fire on a house belonging to a family I knew through an old work colleague; field fires in the heat of summer; and a bomb discovery where building works to create a new housing estate uncovered an old grenade, part of a World War Two munitions site. I attended alarms, where often I was the smallest one so could scramble through a window, chimney fires, chemical incidents and lift rescues. I attended large scale incidents too, including a fire in an airfield where I was involved in using specialist equipment called a

High Volume Pump; a pub fire that grew to a huge scale; and several gutted barns. I also attended many, many more RTCs. I remember being involved with a head-on collision, paramedics pumping units of blood into a male who was clearly bleeding internally and yet had very few visible external injuries. Still when a fairly new firefighter, I remember being in charge of a casualty, finding myself at the head end of the stretcher and therefore giving the commands to move. I remember an elderly couple screaming out in pain, trapped in their vehicle. I remember a young female in her thirties who'd flipped her car with a baby in the back in the middle of the town centre, following a seizure. I remember the air ambulance being called on more than one occasion, and I remember standing on the hard shoulder of the motorway in the early hours of the morning.

Alongside all this were the less pressing engagements. We did drill nights every week, sometimes with the wholetime crew. One of our firefighters was also wholetime at a nearby airport so we had the opportunity to drill there too. We did community events and school visits, Remembrance parades and charity collections. I was proud of my role and still able to box away emotions when needed. It was a reflex now, automatic; adrenaline took over and I reacted instinctively to my training. Most incidents didn't bother me – I hadn't created the situation I was attending, I was just there to help. The damage had already been done. The rest of it, including assisting any casualties, was within my control. If I needed to talk through a job afterwards, I headed to JCs for a cup of tea. On the weeks it wasn't running, the

Community Safety team were based there and someone was usually around. The coordinator of JCs, a firefighter called Joseph, also ran a cadet unit with me. He was always happy to pop the kettle on for a chat.

Then came the next challenge: I needed a full-time job. Being a retained firefighter paid only a part-time wage. I was making ends meet by juggling that with JCs and cadet money, but by this point, I'd moved into a house share with a friend and I needed something more regular. Any new job also had to be something that would allow me to continue to provide on-call day cover. I applied to work as a clinical support worker on the Renal Ward of a hospital, something quite close to my heart. My nan had been a regular patient there for a period of time with kidney failure before she'd passed a few years before.

I went into the job expecting to assist the nurses on the ward, but I was blown away with how amazing my new colleagues were. The nurses generally were all incredibly hard-working, intelligent people, with so many skills to their name. Kidney failure is often caused by different conditions and is particularly linked to diabetes. The staff were hot on it all. Learning about the science behind it, the different types of dialysis and being able to help the doctors in the small procedure room was fascinating. I learnt a lot about empathy from my patients too. Kidney failure means treatment is often needed for the rest of that patient's life, so we had "regulars" in on the ward. I knew the individuals, learnt about their families and their lives at home. Some had missing limbs due to their diabetes, and maintaining their mobility when sick was very tough.

Some had conditions such as schizophrenia and dementia, or suffered hallucinations overnight. Some would have their whole family visiting every day – and some were alone. I tried my best to talk to and connect with every patient. There were general tasks I had to assist them with, such as washing and eating, and it was in that time that I got to know them.

I shadowed the other CSWs initially, who just didn't stop. They seemed to work at a hundred miles an hour and were incredibly in sync with each other. I couldn't have had better role models to show me the ropes. Shifts for me were generally night shifts though, and unfortunately this came at a cost. The human body seems to deteriorate at night, so this was often when the sickest patients passed away. I did my best to support them through that process, and tried to remain with those with no family until death. I was then responsible for assisting the nurses with washing the person who had died and making them presentable for any family members who might arrive, before the body was taken to the morgue. The nurses always talked to the patients, even after death, explaining each task they were about to do, treating them with great dignity and showing an incredible compassion that blew me away.

I was also on hand when patients deteriorated unexpectedly; some kidney failures were acute due to accidents or other illnesses, and some did decline into cardiac arrest. The Renal Ward is where I first put my CPR skills into practice. The deaths I dealt with in the hospital, though, were different to those I experienced from the back of a fire engine. They were generally slower and I was part of the patient's whole care process. After taking time to get to know them, each death was personal. In my head I made a tally, adding each person who passed away to the list as a mark of respect in my own way. I felt they shouldn't die and then be forgotten about. I lost count after the number went past thirty in the first year of my employment.

I often scanned the NHS jobs webpage for any new challenge that might jump out at me. One day a position did just that. Emergency calltakers were being sought for the local ambulance trust, taking 999 calls for an area spanning four counties. The money was a step up from what I was earning as a CSW, it would be shift work instead of permanent nights, and the commute would be thirty minutes rather than the hour I was currently experiencing. It made sense to me, so I applied and was successful. My training started shortly afterwards.

Being a calltaker was a total eye-opener. I undertook several weeks of classroom training and was put through an advanced first aid course, which qualified me to become a co-responder. I was then paired up with a mentor, who shadowed me for twelve full shifts before my assessment to be signed off. The end result was an internationally recognised qualification – and suddenly, a lot of pressure going solo. This was back in 2014. Even then, staffing was stretched and calls were numerous. The phone didn't stop ringing. Working in that job role produced a mix of excitement and terror – some calls gave you an adrenaline rush; some were truly terrible. True to form, my first ever call was regarding a male who was deceased.

I accumulated a vast experience of different

situations very quickly. I instructed callers in giving CPR to patients who weren't breathing; I delivered several babies over the phone. I talked callers through how to help choking family members, and stem their colleagues' blood flow following industrial accidents. I dealt with drowning victims and suicide calls and sick children. Elderly callers would ring first thing in the morning, having had chest pains all night but not wanting to inconvenience anyone. I learnt to stay on the line with lone callers suffering a mental health crisis, sometimes talking to them for over an hour before help arrived, as they were deemed too much of a risk for me to end the call with them. I dealt with burns victims, stroke sufferers, seizures and, of course, more road traffic collisions. My knowledge of the four counties grew better and major roads became familiar. I had a knack for pitching the tone just right to callers, varying between empathic reassurance and stern instruction to keep control of a panicky member of the public.

I was also aware of myself hardening. I put up extra barriers in my mind to protect myself from the influx of calls each time, and I found myself becoming more cynical. I countered this by balancing work with downtime, making sure that when I wasn't on call, I would take the opportunity to do something, drive somewhere, gain a new experience. I kept busy. I also found retreating to the Isle of Wight when on leave was a good coping mechanism to maintain my mental resilience – it seemed to reset my thoughts.

Working for the ambulance service eventually took its toll. Several calls stuck with me and were hard to deal with. Once, I'd just sat down at the start of my shift and the first call I took was from a female. She screamed at me, blaming me because there hadn't been a quick enough response when her brother had fallen and was stuck lying on the floor. He'd had other health complications, and the period of time waiting for an emergency response had resulted in him stopping breathing.

I had a number of calls that required me to give instructions to resuscitate babies. The parents on each occasion were understandably panic-stricken and hysterical, while I tried to tether their focus to my life-saving advice. I dealt with a garden party of elderly friends, all trying to help one of their group who'd collapsed in a cardiac arrest. None of them had the strength to perform compressions effectively and were all taking it in turns to try to help. I had a younger male ring up, refusing to tell me his full name or address but stating that he was about to hang himself. He gave some last messages to me to pass on to his girlfriend, telling me how much he loved her, but he refused to identify himself so I had no house to send an ambulance to. I had the parent of a young child call in, whose daughter had been born with a significant rare health condition and was seriously unwell. No training had prepared me for how to advise the mum. A clinician – a trained paramedic – listened in next to me, also unsure what to say.

All of these added up. Juggling long, demanding shifts alongside being on call was tough. At the same time, my housemate had decided to go travelling, so I needed to find somewhere else affordable to live. This prompted the decision to move closer to work and cut out commuting costs. I ended up moving to a flat in a converted barn in a tiny hamlet just a few minutes away from the ambulance control room. It was the most idyllic place to live. There were even free-roaming peacocks belonging to the farm next door. The downside to this was having to give up my position as an on-call firefighter after three years of service. It was a difficult decision, but ultimately the right one. I moved house in the November and immediately took to country life. I loved being surrounded by fields and having walks on my doorstep, and I found a sense of peace there.

Around the same time, work started to change. The ambulance trust where I was employed altered the system they used to triage with (that is, to assess the nature and severity of a call, then decide on the most appropriate response). The rule was, once you'd completed the training course, you'd be switched over to the new system. From my point of view, this didn't work very well. On one shift, I was the only one who had switched over; as my colleagues had had none of the new training, this made it difficult when I ran into problems. The new system also meant it seemed to take a lot longer to triage callers, and I found calls were starting to queue as the months ticked on. Shift patterns were being experimented with too, morale was poor among the staff and I noticed my own stress levels rising. However, the workplace I was in did tend to have an expiry date. Generally, after a couple of years, calltakers had three possible moves: they could get promoted and moved up; they could slide sideways across to dispatch; or they could leave due to burn out. By the time I was eighteen months into my job, I was the longest-serving calltaker on my team for that reason. I didn't want to become a dispatcher. To me, it felt like playing God, with so many jobs to mobilise to and so few crews to stretch out. I didn't want to be making those decisions on which would take priority. Nor did I want the responsibility of management. I knew something would have to give.

That's when a new opportunity arose.

CHAPTER 3
FIRE CONTROL

Through my colleagues at JCs, I learnt that my county, plus two further brigades, were merging resources and creating one fire control room in an effort to save costs. Had I still lived in my hometown at the time of the vacancy I wouldn't have considered it, as the commute would have been too much. Where I was positioned now, though, was about forty-five miles away: doable, and with a better wage and more regular shifts. I applied and was thrilled to be offered a position, starting in April 2015.

In my eyes, fire control combined my two previous jobs into one and I was excited for the challenge. Looking back, I can see I started a new career in quite a turbulent period of change. My new colleagues were reeling from having had to reapply for their jobs; they'd had to move premises, learn a new mobilising system and essentially deal with triple their previous workload as they took on a further two fire services. I, however, minded none of this and was a little in my element. My knowledge of firefighting and one third of the fire stations already, alongside previous control experience and a good topography of the area, meant it felt as though I was starting ahead. The uncertain times for my new colleagues were preferable to me than the stress levels I'd left behind, so I got stuck into adapting to my new role.

After several weeks of training, I was assigned to Green Watch. My crew members were all incredibly capable and a good example of what I wanted to strive for. My watch manager had had many years of experience, and a couple of newer colleagues, who were still in their development and completing their NVQ qualification, were roughly one year ahead of me in their progress. This helped me enormously as they were able to advise when needed.

I immediately offered to do overtime on the other watches too: each crew had a slightly different way of working, and I wanted to be competent and confident in my job role. The extra money was also helpful. I'd had a taste of adventure during my annual leave over the last couple of years, adhering to my mantra to make the most of every opportunity life handed to me. I'd already taken two weeks in Costa Rica and was keen to visit Canada next, so my extra hours went towards that.

I settled into my new role and I enjoyed it: the pressure was less than my experience with the ambulance service and I had to think outside the box a lot more with specific jobs. As a control operator, or con-op, I was trained in both calltaking and dispatching, and we all worked together on incidents simultaneously. My little hamlet flat had been sold on by my landlord a year after I started my new role, so I'd moved further south in the county too – I was now in a cottage in a slightly bigger village, only half an hour's commute from work. I'd also started instructing for the fire cadet scheme in my new brigade, which was nearer to where I now lived than my previous unit. Things seemed to be going well.

And then.

The 10th August, 2016. I was on my way to work a night shift. My commute at the time involved the particularly nasty A34, which is notorious for collisions. It's a major trunk road spanning a total of three counties. I've always enjoyed driving so this route didn't bother me. I only had four junctions to travel along each time and it was a very familiar road.

This particular evening, though, was incredibly busy, despite being the middle of the week. My carriageway going southbound had heavy traffic. Drivers would start to gain speed then suddenly brake, so I was having to keep my wits about me. I noticed as I crested the hill that the traffic on the northbound side seemed to be stationary, or at least only moving at a crawling pace. I thought first of all that a line of LGVs were in a layby. Then I realised they were waiting in the carriageway. As I started to descend the steep hill, I could see the whole road laid out in front of me – and my attention was caught by a lorry. It was travelling up the hill on the northbound side, going fast. Too fast. It didn't slow down or alter its path, or show in any way that the driver had noticed the stationary vehicles he was rapidly approaching.

I remember looking on helplessly, bracing myself. Should I beep to get his attention, or flash my lights? I somehow knew he wasn't going to stop. I was conscious of being surrounded by heavy traffic and I risked startling the drivers around me, causing my own accident, if I started to sound my horn. Instead I watched, as if seeing it in slow motion, knowing what was about to happen.

The lorry hit the vehicle in front. It had a domino effect: a sports car spun out of the way, trying to get out of its path unsuccessfully and flipping on the verge. A van was crushed. A third vehicle, an estate car, went into a fourth, which vanished under a second lorry. Two further lorries were in front of that. Eight vehicles were involved in total, and the point of impact happened just as I was passing in lane two – they smashed level with my shoulder. The noise was indescribable. It totally encompassed my car and made me jump hard in my seat. I swore, and I remember clutching the steering wheel in a death grip, my whole body tensed.

I looked back in my wing mirror at the devastation as my car continued. I watched the back trailer doors of the second lorry buckling and it being pushed up off its rear wheels as the last car was shunted under it. I couldn't stop. There was nowhere to pull over on my side of the dual carriageway. I couldn't even call it in to my colleagues on 999. My phone was hidden deep in the pockets of my bag on the floor and I couldn't reach it. So, with no other option, I continued my commute, shaking for most of the way.

I got to work earlier than my colleagues, which was usual. By the time they arrived, my shaking had subsided and my breathing had calmed down. We were passed the incident on handover and I mentioned that I'd witnessed it happen, all the while keeping myself in check. Our station manager at the time attended the crash in an officer capacity; he went home via the control room to see us all. On finding out that I'd driven past the scene as the RTC had occurred, he chatted to me briefly in his office. He confirmed details of the collision and offered to show me photos taken for investigation purposes. Quite often, particularly within Control, it's very easy for gaps in a story to be filled in with imaginings for our brains to gain a full picture. I wanted to see the photos. I wanted to compare them with what I was sure I'd seen in that split second of passing, but which somehow seemed too terrible to be true.

My memory and experience of the crash tallied totally with what he showed me. The scene was horrific. Despite this, I was glad to have seen the pictures and to be able to absorb them properly. The station manager asked me if I was ok and I confirmed that I was. He also suggested I ring the police non-emergency line to provide my details as a witness. I agreed to do that once my shift had ended.

I was on the primary 9s position for that shift. That meant I was first port of call whenever the emergencies rang in. It also meant I had almost nothing to do with radio messages and liaising directly with crews on ongoing incidents. Every role is incorporated in the same room and everyone works simultaneously on incidents, but we tend to keep to our allocated roles of calltaker, radio operator or answering admin lines to avoid confusion when the room becomes busy. We rotate these roles on a shift-by-shift basis to keep up competencies and vary our jobs. Being on primary 9s for this particular night shift, however, was very difficult. The A34 incident was still open and messages were drip fed from the crews as the night progressed. I sat for fifteen hours, watching as the log was amended throughout the night. I knew that, logically, it would make no difference to the outcome if I took a message or if a colleague did. But doing nothing increased my feeling of being out of control and of catastrophe building. I was incredulous that my watch seemed so indifferent to this crash. To them, although a nasty one, it was just another RTC and they kept themselves at their professional emotional distance. I, however, felt overwhelmed by it. I withdrew into myself, trying to act normally, while inside crumbling as more and more was learnt about the situation.

By 08:30hrs the following morning, the incident was finally completed and the remaining casualties had been extricated from the vehicle. These, sadly, were those who hadn't survived. It was confirmed that four people had lost their lives that evening, and one more was in a serious condition in hospital. The deceased persons were an adult female and three children, all of whom were in the car crushed beneath the articulated lorry.

CHAPTER 4
AFTERWARDS

I went home after that shift to call the police and provide my statement. I told them what I knew over the phone and passed on my contact details. They arranged for an officer to come to my house a couple of days later to take a formal statement.

My journey home was difficult. I cried heavily as I passed the scene of what had taken place just hours before. Debris was still visible, strewn along the verge. I didn't sleep as I would usually have done between night shifts. Instead, since by now the story had exploded in the media, I couldn't help but seek out further details.

I found myself searching out every article. I learnt the names and faces of those who had been killed; a mother and her two sons, and her partner's daughter. Her partner and his son were in the car directly behind, and the two vehicles had been forced into each other. I felt stricken to think of the poor survivors of that family, watching the car in front of them go under the trailer. I also noted the driver of the lorry, who'd caused the crash, had been arrested. I didn't know what to think about him. He was clearly driving too fast and was obviously distracted right until the last minute, as he made no attempt to avoid the traffic or slow down. And yet, he was a normal person. He drove dangerously but he didn't climb into his cab that morning determined to kill a family. How many people in life can honestly say they've never driven while distracted? I felt torn. I wanted to hate him yet somehow was unable to.

I read about the other seriously injured person too – the driver of the sports car that was struck first, who saw the lorry approaching and tried to move his vehicle out of its path. He was currently fighting for his life after being airlifted to hospital. So much destruction in just one moment blew my mind.

My next night shift ended uneventfully. I cried again travelling that same stretch of road, in both directions, before and after my shift. I fell into bed exhausted when I got home but my sleep was disrupted and I had nightmares. This was new to me – I'd often had vivid dreams but very rarely did I suffer from nightmares. I was aware that it was normal to have an acute stress reaction after experiencing trauma, so I didn't really pay much attention to my body's response. I did notice that I was emotional, very up and down, in the days that followed. I told family and some close friends that I'd witnessed the crash but didn't specify details. I painted an almost upbeat picture to them to show I was all right, emphasising the irony of my luck that of course it was me who'd been passing that road at that particular time. I found myself deflecting questions about the crash or queries into my welfare, and kept conversations about it at a surface level.

A police officer came to take my statement just a few days later. He asked for every detail I could remember, from the weather conditions, to lane positions, to the colour of each vehicle involved. He also asked for my car's details, as there were several dashcams that had recorded footage from various perspectives. As my car at the time was a distinctive green hatchback, it would easily be spotted on the footage handed in. I noted that the police officer was clearly trying to hide how angry he was about the circumstances of the crash, although he didn't provide any details for me, nor did I ask. He was very professional and breached no confidentialities. However, his disguised emotion and the nature of how the driver was travelling led me to suspect he was on his mobile phone. I was told I would be kept informed of any updates; if the driver pleaded not guilty then it would go to court and the potential would be there for me to be called up as a witness. If he pleaded guilty, that wouldn't be necessary but I'd get an update letter sent to me with the result.

The next few weeks passed and the nightmares continued: I'd dream of family members dying; of car crashes; of having to choose which ones to save when faced with multiple loved ones unresponsive. I even dreamt of my parents' dog dying and had to check on him the next morning. Sleeping patterns were erratic and I seemed to have lost something; some spark within. I'd always been able to rationalise the incidents I'd dealt with in the past. But this was a car full of kids and I'd watched it happen. I couldn't get past that; that out-of-control feeling. And a feeling of guilt for not having been able to intervene.

I remained very up and down when at home. When in company, I forced away my emotional state and hardened my exterior to protect myself. But I still cried each time I passed the crash site when I travelled to work.

Then came October 2016. A couple of things happened: first, the lorry driver pleaded guilty to four counts of causing death by dangerous driving, and one count of causing serious injury by dangerous driving. He was sentenced to ten years in prison. It was revealed that the crash was caused because he was scrolling through the music on his phone continuously, not looking up until less than a second before impact and failing to apply the brakes at all. He was travelling at 50mph. He had signed an agreement just that morning with the company he drove for stating he agreed not to use his mobile phone while behind the wheel. All this explained the emotions I read in the police officer's expression when providing my statement.

A video was also released by the local police that month. It was footage of the collision from inside the lorry cab, showing the reaction of the driver and the full devastation laid out before him. It also showed the surviving family members giving statements. They described their lost loved ones and made a plea to people not to use a mobile phone when driving. It was a powerful, moving video, and one that I simultaneously couldn't cope with watching, yet couldn't draw myself away from. The footage showed my car quite clearly and just how close I was to it all. The family statements turned the victims into real people; just innocent children and a mother who loved them. It was effective in its message and devastating to watch.

As time moved on, I felt there was partial closure, for me, at least. The criminal proceedings were over and the media coverage died down. My own reaction calmed somewhat too – the nightmares eased off and my tears dried up. I still thought about the crash every day, particularly as I had to commute the A34 most days, but otherwise I was once again able to raise the carefully created barriers I'd worked so hard to form over the years.

At work, I was coming to the end of my NVQ process – this meant a substantial pay rise from my development pay to now being competent in my role. With recent events still so fresh in my mind, it stiffened my resolve to make the most of every day. I also wanted to regain some normality and keep myself busy. Good friends of mine, Sasha and her husband, had just taken over responsibilities for a Portuguese villa that had been in their family a long time, and had offered a small group of friends the opportunity to go and experience "Portuguese time" with them. I went along at the end of November into December, as part of a working party of five to help out with the maintenance of the grounds. I had the most enjoyable time, letting off steam with a mixture of being shown the sights, stripping back the grounds, which had become overgrown because the bungalow had been unoccupied, and cutting down trees. There was downtime too, exploring the beaches and the local beauty spots.

As it was winter, each evening we retreated into the property, with an open fire, a few drinks between us, crossword challenges and lots of laughter. It was a tonic for me. On the back of it I decided, with the increase in my wages, to explore more of the world. So, I made a New Year's resolution: to visit a different country every month for a year, mainly short city breaks for a couple of nights at a time that I could fit in on my rota days off between shifts.

I made a booking and researched every detail I wanted to explore, from landmarks to places to eat.

My first destination? Prague.

CHAPTER 5
TRAVEL

January came round and it was time for my trip. I chose Prague for my first solo venture as it's a reputedly safe city, and small enough for everything to be within walking distance. I love taking photos and enjoy wandering and getting lost, capturing everything that that entails. I tend to avoid public transport for that reason – it takes away the fun of making a wrong turn!

I'd looked into everything beforehand and planned each detail meticulously, trying to group close landmarks together to create a logical route. I found it thrilling and freeing to be absorbing so many new things; exploring somewhere totally unknown to me. It was empowering to do it by myself. I love history and trying local cuisine, and standing at stunning viewpoints just to take the world in. I'm a fan of extremes of weather too, so I was excited to discover snow on the ground at -11°C. I found the break a perfect distraction from my own thoughts. I was up early every morning to walk and find breakfast. I completed full days of sightseeing and crashed into bed every night, exhausted. It reset my mind; provided respite from my racing thoughts over the last few months and continued what my trip to Portugal had started for my wellbeing.

I came home from Prague with stories to tell, a thirst to travel more, and a knowledge of how to keep the A34 out of my head: if I kept busy and distracted, everything else was manageable.

After Prague followed Bergen in February, then Copenhagen in March. I'd found a real zeal in my mini-breaks and I loved to plan ahead for the next trip. Norway was beautiful and I vowed I'd visit Scandinavia to see the Northern Lights one day. I climbed a mountain via cable car and ate reindeer and lots of local fish. I also got chatting to people on a boat tour of the fjords, particularly a lovely American couple who happened to be staying in the UK and were exploring more of Europe while they had the opportunity. I ended up having dinner with them that evening and we stayed in touch afterwards, which was an unexpected bonus to the trip. Solo travelling was bringing out a new type of confidence in me – to actively approach strangers and engage in conversations, quite frequently coming away with new friends.

From Bergen, I flew straight into Copenhagen, where I stayed in a hotel room overlooking the harbour of Nyhavn. I toured the palaces and castles in awe, found the local must-see tourist sites, and discovered a street market with lots of different food that I kept returning to.

After the double trip, I returned home exhausted and satisfied, but also realising that two trips back-to-back was perhaps a little too much!

April brought me to Amsterdam. I had a very cultural exploration of this city. I queued up for four hours to tour the house of Anne Frank; seeing it for myself was a thought-provoking experience. I explored the museums of Salvador Dali, Banksy and Vincent Van Gogh. I booked a coach trip for a day to look at the tulip fields and gazed in wonder over acres and acres of flowers. I took an afternoon to visit the windmills, and another to travel across to experience the A'DAM tower, including having a go on the swing mounted on the top of the tower overlooking the whole city.

By this point, I was feeling more like myself again. As long as I kept busy and didn't think about it, everything stayed buried. I'd get home with more stories to tell and photos to show. Work colleagues had become invested too, advising me where to go next and what to do on my travels. As soon as the high of the last trip started to fade, I'd be looking forward to the next one.

I wanted to visit Italy on my travels, so May took me to Naples. The scorching weather made me happy immediately and gave me the excuse to sample all the ice cream flavours I could. I also visited a specific pizza restaurant, which only had a choice of two pizzas on the menu, but was so renowned it had people queueing down the street for tables. As a solo visitor, I was plonked at a table with another lone individual – a girl from the States – and we shared travel experiences. Amongst other things, this trip meant I could visit Pompeii – making another new travel buddy in the process – and then climb Vesuvius. The history of both places, and the incredible views, made the trip for me.

My year continued like this. From Naples, I was invited back to Portugal with my friends and had another wonderful time with them at their home-from-home. Then came Switzerland, where I travelled from Geneva to a tiny village next to a lake in a mountainous range only accessible via cable car. August took me to Budapest. I stayed there in a famous spa hotel and enjoyed the outdoor pool in the beautiful sun every morning, before the weather became blazing hot.

September was a little different, in the form of a family holiday for all five of us, something we hadn't done for many years. We went to Menorca, which was lovely, but it was meant to be a slower-paced, relaxing holiday. However, my mindset at that point had not yet reached relaxed. I found my sister frustrating but my family, still used to living with one another, couldn't see anything wrong. I was perceived as making things awkward. Admittedly I had rather a short fuse just then, and it didn't take much for me to become annoyed or sharp with them. The holiday was pleasant but I felt a little fraught too, and was glad to return once our time away was up.

I received a call from my mum later that week – she and my dad had noticed I was withdrawn and not myself. She told me they thought I should see a doctor and suggested I had depression. I was touched that they'd noticed my mood was off, but also somewhat insulted. I wasn't depressed. I knew that for certain. I felt plenty of joy when gallivanting on my own for my other trips.

But I'd watched several people die in front of me in a catastrophic way just a year previously, and was trying to come to terms with that and to manage life as normally as I could. I felt that I was a different me – separated from everyone else by something huge they could never understand. The seemingly trivial undertakings of my family that week had made me realise how divided I felt from them. It wasn't personal. I knew deep down that any falling-out really was my fault for somehow not being able to tolerate them all of a sudden. But a long week in close proximity to them for the first time really since the crash (barring popping in for cups of tea for a couple of hours at a time) was really rather difficult. And that wasn't something I'd anticipated.

I assured my parents that I wasn't depressed, I just had a lot on. But I thanked them for their concern. I also promised myself I'd bottle things better in front of them in the future. I loved them all and didn't want to worry them; nor did I want to deal with questions I couldn't face the answers to. I'd reached a fairly stable position and didn't want to jeopardise that.

I returned to the Isle of Wight for my October trip. I needed my familiar breathing space and funds were also a little tight that month. I delighted in being on the beach in my wellies, and exploring my old haunts in the down season with no tourists to hinder me. Once more, I revelled in my own company.

November took me to Athens for a cultural

holiday. I made lots of historical visits and was caught in a biblical storm that caused flash flooding to the centre of the city. Then in December, as planned, I went to Berlin – where else was there to go for a Christmas market but Germany? I split my time there exploring the many mulled wines and Christmas trees there were throughout the city, and taking some educational trips too, including a visit to the concentration camp of Sachsenhausen.

The end of that mini-break was bitter sweet – the twelve-month challenge I'd set myself was at an end, and I knew reality wasn't far behind.

I worked the week leading up to Christmas and I distinctly remember a few nasty jobs in a row. We had three persons deceased in separate RTCs, and also a male discovered hanging following his suicide, all in the one week. I remember being a little snappy with my crew manager at the time, as she was insisting on covering a training topic she'd left to the last minute, before our rota days off. I thought it was disrespectful and not appropriate to be cramming it in when we'd been dealing with persons just declared dead, and at Christmas too – just because she hadn't organised her schedule. She replied with some astonishment that she didn't think I'd be bothered or affected by that sort of thing. Her response made me wonder. Was I more upset than I should have been? Than my colleagues were? Or was it just because it was Christmas, or her lack of organisation that it wound me up? In any case, I said no more about it, swallowed a retort and the tears I could feel burning, and completed the training as she requested.

The following year dawned and I had a renewed

sense of purpose as the next challenge arose to focus on. As much as I absolutely loved the little cottage I currently lived in, and the village life that went with it, I decided I needed to save to buy my first place. It was finally time to get onto the property ladder. I gave myself two years; that was how long I had left on my lease, and I rose to the challenge. Every overtime shift I was available to take, every JCs' session or cadet night I could attend, I did so. I opened a savings account and worked hard to be able to watch the amount build. It had a dual effect too: it kept me busy and the momentum stopped me thinking too much.

My downtime was also spent wisely. I used days off to catch up with friends, see the family, and take long daytrips to go walking or to the beach, clearing my mind with no expense except fuel and the odd bag of fish and chips. I tried to work on my physical fitness too, which had somewhat declined since giving up being a retained firefighter. I joined a fitness class based on a farm, throwing tyres, lifting logs and dragging bits of farm equipment around the field, and I loved it. I also focused on my eating habits and tried to improve those too. I rarely had a day at home by myself to do nothing, and I preferred it that way. My cottage had a log burner, which I adored, and unwinding with a glass of wine in front of the fire after a busy day ensured exhaustion and a peaceful night's sleep.

By the summer of 2018, I was getting itchy feet again and had over a fortnight booked off as leave. I figured, after all my travelling in Europe the previous year, it would make sense to explore more of the UK. It would be a more affordable trip too to work alongside my saving goals. I set myself a challenge to plan a two-week road trip spanning the length of the UK, starting up in John O'Groats and winding my way down to Land's End by the end of the fortnight. I also planned a three-day break before that to Wales with a couple of friends.

The trip to Wales was beautifully scenic, and it was good to catch up with two best mates I'd known for years, Beth and Georgia. Georgia was the housemate I used to share with. However, by the end of the mini-trip, I was champing at the bit for some peace and time to myself again.

Something had changed within me. I had always been a sociable person but I was discovering that I now had a limited tolerance of other people's company. I seemed to find it rather wearisome to endure anyone for a prolonged period of time. I craved being alone and yet, when I *was* alone, I needed to reach out and do something; be with someone. It felt like a hard balance to achieve.

I came home after that trip to Wales, packed my car, and then left at 04:00hrs the following day to begin the arduous journey up to the top of Scotland. This was during a heatwave, and I hoped it would continue as I'd be camping throughout the whole trip. Alas, on arrival at John O'Groats that evening, it was raining heavily. Nevertheless I was excited, and the sight and smell of the sea had renewed my enthusiasm after so many hours stuck in the car by myself. I pitched my tent and had to laugh – I had specifically brought with me a small, one-man, pop-up tent, typically the type used in festivals. I knew I'd be staying in a new place every night and it would be convenient; four pegs and guy lines and it was done. It looked tiny compared to the other tents surrounding mine, and of course the single skin would be tested in the torrential downpour! I went to find some food, then settled for the night, quickly learning that as long as I didn't lean on the sides of the tent, I would actually remain dry.

The whole fortnight was a thrill. I got into a routine: I'd have some breakfast, get on the road for two to three hours to my next destination, spend the rest of the day exploring, and then tuck down into the night's campsite. I spent four nights in Scotland, including a day and second night in John O' Groats. I drove through the Highlands and slept next to Loch Ness, visiting Inverness and Aberdeen, and of course Edinburgh. I then picked my way through Newcastle to the Lake District, down through York and into the Yorkshire Dales. The Peak District and Gloucester led me down to Devon and finally into Cornwall.

I tried to do as many of the touristy things as I could, including visiting lots of castles. I tried to eat the local delicacies too: plenty of haggis in Scotland – I even had a deep-fried Mars bar – and I made sure to enjoy a cream tea in both Devon and Cornwall to, of course, compare the two. I loved the challenge of constantly changing surroundings; of driving the whole distance by myself and amending my plans around any whims or spur-of-the-moment stops. I also updated my social media as I went, and my friends again got on board, offering suggestions of places to eat or things to do. It seemed the perfect balance of finding pleasure in company but not being engulfed by it. I chatted to strangers and met people to talk to at each campsite, touching base with friends and family along my journey. But if I wanted to go off-grid, that was also easily achievable. The experience was very reminiscent of my European mini-travels and I didn't want it to end.

But obviously, everything does. I returned home and quickly got back into the swing of overtime and a very busy life. Work continued in much the same way as it always had, until the October – when I was given notice that I'd be changing watches and moving across to White Watch. After nearly four years of working with the same people, this would be a new challenge for me. But I tried to embrace it.

White Watch came as a bit of a shock. I wasn't the only person to have moved. In fact, the watch had been shaken up to balance competencies and certain events taking place, resulting in an almost brand-new watch of very different characters. We didn't gel; we weren't in sync; and it took several months for that balance to be achieved and for us to work together well.

I struggled a lot with the fact that many hours would pass without any conversation. The tension and silence to me were deafening. After several weeks of this, I became rather tearful. I lived alone, which meant I didn't chat on my downtime, only to get to work to find the same lack of conversation. I spoke to the station manager, who assured me that a couple more moves would be taking place in the new year and the atmosphere would become easier. I waited impatiently, in the meantime starting to dread the workspace that, until that point, had become a kind of coping mechanism for me.

When 2019 arrived, so did two more members of staff – thank goodness. This changed the dynamic again but this time for the better. We chatted more and eventually, in the months to come, we became the kind of strong watch I was used to working with. I learnt never to take my colleagues for granted; we spent too many hours in our workplace to be unhappy.

The rest of my year was fairly uneventful. I continued to save as much money as I could and still undertook a lot of overtime shifts. I managed two last-minute breaks away: a short trip to Fuerteventura at the end of January and a cheap holiday to Greece in the summer. My January trip was desperately needed – for some reason, I felt incredibly stressed out, likely because of the stresses I was feeling at work with my new watch. I also had a continuous cough and cold that I couldn't seem to shift, and I figured I was getting run down. Some winter sunshine and a break from everything would remedy that, I thought. My germs did eventually shift.

As the year went on, I started to focus my attention on buying my first home. I viewed lots of places, being fairly flexible on where I'd go, depending on my budget. Closer to work meant more expensive; further north in the county was closer to family but a longer commute. I finally chose to move sideways, settling on a place in the next county. It was approximately forty minutes from work – a doable commute on a motorway but being in another postcode meant it was cheaper. Although it would mean being an hour from my nearest close friends and ninety minutes' drive from my family, I figured it was a step onto the ladder. I could drive to visit family on my days off and I'd be quite happy meeting new people as I went along.

The flat I'd found was in a converted malthouse, with beams and period features, situated in a small market town. It seemed the perfect fit and, as the purchase progressed, I became increasingly excited for my new adventure.

CHAPTER 6
COVID-19

As 2020 got underway, my flat purchase was still dragging on. There were legal complications because it was leasehold. I finally got an approximate completion date for the end of February, when I would collect the keys. My move itself would be a little staggered – my cottage rental contract expired in March, so I would have nearly a month in which to address a few issues within the flat, before moving my belongings in and actually transferring over. I collected the keys at last on 28th February 2020, after a tense day of waiting while at JCs for word that things were finalised and the flat was mine. Once I got that call, I dashed over to claim it. I set about arranging for electrics to be updated and ceilings plastered. I also got on with some of the painting before my furniture filled the place up. I was on a high – my flat was quirky and I enjoyed being at the start of making it my own. I discovered a love for decorating and painting, and it was another project I could sink my teeth into to distract myself.

I booked the removals van and moved in properly on 21st March.

Two days later, on 23rd March 2020, the country shut down.

Coronavirus had hit. It had been an uncertain few weeks, with tensions mounting across the UK. Even my removals guys refused to shake hands but instead offered an elbow to "tap" in greeting. It was all very strange and almost a joke first of all. I never truly believed that a full lockdown could happen. How could you just stop a country from functioning? I listened to Boris Johnson's announcement, full of dread. It was declared that the lockdown would be for two weeks. We weren't to go out unless strictly necessary: for essential work or medical care, for necessary shopping, to get some exercise once a day.

I couldn't believe my bad luck. I was in a new flat, in a new town, in a new county. I had no one around me and the place where I now lived still felt like the home of a stranger. And now I was confined to it.

I cried a lot that day. In an instant – in the space of one speech – almost my entire world had stopped. I couldn't see my family or my friends. Not even a doorstep visit was an option as they were all too far away. JCs and cadets all stopped too. The goal I'd been striving towards for over two years and one of my proudest achievements – buying my own flat on my own merit – was overshadowed by a pandemic unlike anything else. I couldn't share my new place with anyone. Instead, I had to deal with the crippling isolation that was handed to me, coupled with an intense fear that my vulnerable mum would catch this deadly virus. Stories in the media showed the devastating effects of Covid, and the death count rose higher every day.

My only saving grace was Control. Emergencies still happened. Working from home wasn't possible for us, so I was allowed to go into work each day. My watch were the only people I interacted with face-to-face for ten long weeks: because of course, the initial lockdown fortnight was extended over and over again.

I was incredibly low. I'd cry in the car on the way to work and then return to an empty flat. Where I would normally chat with friends, and with those at JCs when anything particularly nasty came through on my shifts, instead I returned to silence. My days off each week became stagnant; futile. It took all my energy to shower and eat, because honestly, what was the point? I'd never felt so incredibly lonely in all my life. My family didn't seem to understand; life continued almost in the same way for them. My sister, who'd moved out herself by this point, did struggle somewhat – she was furloughed from her job so was now stuck at home. However, she was local to my family and could still do doorstep visits to them and to her friends. She also took the time to throw herself into her cooking, a passion of hers.

My brother still lived with our parents and benefitted from the lockdown, as it meant he could now work from home; he was able to save all the money he'd normally spend on commuting, and was doing well by it. As for my parents, their lives stayed almost the same. My dad, being semi-retired, continued his part-time deliveries and my mum's schedule didn't alter. Other than having to queue in shops and remarking on the empty grocery aisles, plus having fewer visits from their kids, their worlds just didn't change very much. My dad, on one of our video calls, expressed surprise that I was upset. He said I seemed to be taking the lockdown to heart and that I should just try to get on with it. There was no malice in his comment and no insult intended, but my lockdown life was a world away from the one they were experiencing.

My life became either work or sitting on the sofa at home. I didn't have a lot of motivation or inclination to do much else. I booked in more overtime shifts; a poor way to socialise and have something to do but I didn't care. I was just desperate to see and speak to other people. My normal life schedule pre-Covid didn't stop – I always made sure I was as busy as possible – only now I was trying to cope with the exact opposite of the way I'd been living. Even at work I became very withdrawn. My colleagues would discuss the pandemic and how terrible it was; how they missed doing certain things or seeing particular loved ones. Yet nearly all of them then went back home to their families at the end of the day. The few individuals who lived alone like me still had their support networks in their towns around them. My house move was extremely bad timing and left me desperate.

However, I also felt a kind of guilt for struggling so much. My physical health was good and I wasn't vulnerable to the likes of this virus; nobody I knew personally had lost their life because of the illness; I could still work and my flat purchase had completed in time for me to have a stable roof over my head. I wasn't in the habit of self-pity and I chastised myself for it; I desperately wanted my usual attitude of being able to put on a brave face and box things up. I would try to be stoic in front of my colleagues – most of my tears were reserved for when I was alone, hence a lot of car-crying. But with my usual coping mechanisms having been taken away from me, it was inordinately difficult.

Easter 2020 was the only time I bent Boris's new rules slightly. I purchased a pet: a Continental Giant house rabbit, whom I named Bertie. I collected him from a breeder who lived one junction up the motorway from where I was. Technically, with the restrictions in place, I probably shouldn't have got him when I did. In my eyes though, he was very much an essential purchase. Bertie was the reason I needed to get up at a certain time each morning; he was destructive and surprisingly vocal when his breakfast wasn't fed to him when he was expecting it. He was also affectionate and soppy; was something I could focus on. And he was company, another living being in my space – and although he didn't say much, he made a massive difference.

Bertie lived in the spare bedroom but would have free roam of the flat. As I was at home a lot, he was well used to being handled, and was full of sass and attitude that made me laugh. My social media, once exciting and full of travels, was now flooded with rabbit photos. Bertie was the only new thing I had to discuss in my life, and sharing his antics was a way of reaching out for human contact from my loved ones, without expressly shouting, *Help Me*. I knew everyone was struggling in their own way, so I tried hard not to moan or burden others with how lonely and sad I felt. Instead, I channelled my energies into Bertie and tried to just carry on.

VE Day commemorations were held in May to celebrate seventy-five years since the end of WWII. I desperately craved to be involved in the street parties that took place everywhere; people sitting in their front gardens and sharing the event with neighbours. My block of flats didn't take part in this, nor did anybody in my road. To make matters worse, my family all got together in my parents' front garden, then video called me so they could say hi. I felt wretched. I knew they were just trying to include me, but I was trying so hard to keep it together, knowing they were having a lovely family time and I wasn't allowed to go and join them. It heightened my feelings of loneliness and I really struggled that day. The tears continued to flow.

As summer arrived, rules started to relax a little. I longed for the garden I used to have with my rental cottage, as my new flat had no land with it. Still, the lessening of restrictions and the company of Bertie the bunny gave me a little more strength of mind – and the opportunity to shop again was now there, with more premises opening. So, I set about organising the flat. I finished the painting, did a cheap refurb of the kitchen and bathroom, and got carpets fitted throughout.

Masks were now mandatory in public. This was a big U-turn, as we'd previously been told they were ineffective. I suffer from a skin condition that ironically flares under stress. At that point, my face was so bad it hurt to lay my head down on my pillow at night. No way could I tolerate having material pressed to my skin in the form of a mask, so I was exempt. Strangely, this was another stressor. Other people hated the fact that I wasn't wearing a mask, despite my wearing an exemption lanyard and keeping my distance. And actually, it was only very recently that having to wear one *wasn't* in the rules at all. Also, wearing a face covering seemed to make others feel invincible, as some conveniently forgot about personal space, making me quite anxious as they edged closer to me in shopping queues.

Although it was still advised to be outdoors to reduce exposure, we were eventually allowed to travel to see people. I remember one day in particular sometime in August, when I visited my hometown. I caught up with three friends individually outside, then had a doorstep visit with my parents. After seeing them all, I felt considerably lighter. It seemed, perhaps, that we were working our way out of this horrible situation, and I was hopeful.

The 12th October 2020 was the next hurdle for me. We received a call into work: an RTC. A car had hit a lorry head on and it was reported that there was a family inside: two parents and four children. The youngest child, just a baby, had been ejected from the vehicle. I took the call, being in the primary 9s position that shift. I knew this job wasn't good and sure enough, the outcome was devastating. The mother was pronounced dead on scene, as were two of the older children. The third died in hospital that same night. Only the baby and the father survived this horrific ordeal. We had records of this particular family. It turned out they'd suffered a house fire only months previously at the beginning of lockdown. My heart went out to the dad. He'd lost his home and then nearly his whole family in less than a year.

This job shook me. I didn't take my break on that shift; I couldn't pull myself away from it. It was reminiscent of the crash those few years ago in 2016, with lorries and innocent children yet again involved. I fought to remain composed but with no reserve left in me to do so. I must have been visibly struggling as I received a couple of messages from very kind work friends, checking in on me the following day.

I ended up doing what I did all those years ago: following the media stories and reading everything I could to find out about this family and this crash. I didn't sleep. My sleeping pattern over the next few days, already erratic as I'd struggled to drop off every night since the pandemic had started, now became broken and punctured with old nightmares again. My managers at the time arranged trauma support for us all for the next week. This is when a trauma support volunteer (these are trained members of staff from across all departments of the brigade) comes in and talks the watch through events after a particularly traumatic job, checking on our welfare and helping us gain a clearer picture of the whole story, with the intention of laying the job to rest in our minds. Sometimes, attending officers will also join the session to give their insight. It answered some questions for me – why the crash came about in the first place, for example – but it didn't stop me running events in my mind over and over again, nor did it solve my sleeping issues.

I was just beginning to feel "normal" again after that most recent crash – as normal as I was used to feeling in the middle of a pandemic – when the government announced a second lockdown for the beginning of November. My world fell apart. This one was scheduled to last for four weeks, but the March lockdown was supposed to have been a fortnight, yet was extended to two and a half months. I immediately fell into the dark, lonely situation I'd been in earlier in the year; sometimes tearful at work and feeling helpless at home. The one change to this lockdown was that individuals living by themselves were allowed to "bubble" with someone else. My Covid bubble was with my sister, as she was also on her own. However, between my work and hers – which had since resumed – we only met up once. It was nice to be able to be with her properly indoors and to share a meal, but the physical distance between us didn't really make the bubble work. Thankfully, by the first week of December, lockdown restrictions were once again eased. Everyone held their breath for Christmas.

As it turned out, Christmas was the luck of the draw dependent on which tier you were living in at the time. I felt awful for my colleagues and friends who had planned Christmas with loved ones, only for the government to put restrictions on them right at the last minute. Thankfully, from a selfish point of view, I was allowed to continue with my plans with my family: we were permitted to mingle for the one day, with restrictions back in place for Boxing Day. Even more luckily, my work shifts for 2020 meant I had Christmas Day off. I drove to my hometown and spent it with my family, feeling incredibly fortunate to be able to do so, and empathising so much with those who couldn't be with theirs.

The first week in January 2021 brought the third and final lockdown to the UK. I was beside myself at this point. I had barely coped with November and this third one had no foreseeable end date. Cases of Covid were skyrocketing after the country had reunited with their families for the festive celebrations. So I used this latest announcement to make a decision: I would sell my flat and move back closer to loved ones. I couldn't cope with continual lockdowns and I needed to do something before I broke. My flat went on the market a couple of weeks later.

Estate agents at the time were operating, but with severe restrictions. I couldn't view any houses until my flat had an offer in place, and people viewing the flat had to be ready to buy. I also had the tricky situation that most people, like me, were selling due to the effects of the pandemic. A lot of buyers were looking for properties with gardens, having been through a lockdown heatwave without one. I got lucky, however; my flat was looking better since I'd decorated and a couple of first-time buyers fell in love with it. I accepted an offer in April, and three weeks later found a new house to purchase. It was back in my hometown; a ridiculous commute to work that I once wouldn't even have considered. But as I had a different perspective now, having endured a lot of isolation, the driving became a compromise I suddenly wasn't concerned about. Like the flat, this house was also very much a doer-upper, needing decorating and revamping throughout. I didn't mind though – all I wanted was a garden, a real fireplace and to be nearer to my family and friends. This little mid-terraced house ticked all those boxes and was being sold empty, so there was no chain to speak of.

Lockdown number three also coincided with other changes. Early in the year, before my house move, I was yet again required to move watches at work, this time to Blue Watch to balance out competencies. Blues were lovely and very welcoming, but I felt as though I'd had the carpet pulled out from under me a little. White Watch had been my only stable support network during the most trying time of my life so far, yet now I felt I was being ripped away from them too. I understood why the move had to take place, but I couldn't help but feel the timing was all wrong, and almost dangerous for me.

By this point, work colleagues were voicing concerns about my wellbeing to Sam, my station manager and Keith, my group manager. Keith in particular seemed to be keeping an eye; we'd had several chats in his office on how I was coping, and he also had a word with HR regarding the number of hours I was working. Staff members generally are restricted in the amount of overtime they can undertake, for their own wellbeing. However, Keith knew that being at work right now was the only thing keeping me sane, and he relaxed that rule for me. I was incredibly grateful for this and threw myself into working more than ever. I hated being locked in at home.

I had a new Covid bubble this time – my friend Lucy and her husband-to-be were happy to take me under their wing. They lived just shy of an hour away from my flat, and I ended up having weekly dinners with them. Their extended families liked doing quizzes and playing games via video call with each other, and soon I was involved in that too. I even had a virtual cider festival with them all and stayed overnight, along with Bertie in his travel crate. Those friends honestly both saved my sanity and I owe them everything. Lucy is the daughter of my friend Sasha and they happen to live on the same estate, so I got to have doorstep meet-ups with her too when I visited.

Lockdown was still in full swing in February, my birthday month. I was to turn thirty, and before Covid I'd had grand plans of going somewhere snowy and searching out the Northern Lights. Instead, I was stuck inside a flat I considered a prison at this point, with no one to share the day with. My Covid bubble had celebrated with me the week before, making me an amazing cake and gifting me a large box of thirty individually wrapped presents from themselves and Sasha too.

I'd booked an overtime night shift for the actual night of my thirtieth, just so as to have some company and social interaction on my big birthday. I cried most of the day, feeling rather sorry for myself, even though I received so many calls and texts that day into the evening, and felt so very loved. My family had already posted me some beautiful birthday gifts, and my parents paid for a meal to be delivered to me too, which was a wonderful thought and a delicious birthday lunch. Yet, somehow, I still felt so alone.

Once I got to work, I had another nice surprise – Green Watch were lovely and knew just what I was doing by being there. They'd got me a card and a cake for the occasion, which made me cry some more.

In March a work friend, Amy, became very poorly. She only lived in the next town on from me and we were good friends in work, but she'd always kept herself to herself in her downtime so we'd never really socialised out of the workplace before. Her crew manager, a mutual friend, advised her to call me for some support and help with collecting her medications from a pharmacy, as she was currently unable to travel herself. Amy had always been reluctant to bother anyone for anything so I know it took her a lot of courage, but she did ring me and I was so glad. She was very distressed and we had a long chat. Then I collected the items she needed plus a few other bits to keep her going while she was unwell, and popped round.

She really was quite poorly and under investigation for various things, which took a toll on her mentally too. I tried my best to support her, and sneaked her a care package in hospital when she was admitted a few weeks later. I was honoured she'd trusted me enough to ask for help, and pleased I could do something for her. Her illness also kept my own loneliness at bay a little, and gave me a purpose. She was off sick for a few months and I tried to be a shoulder for her in that time. I'd have garden visits with her and would bring Bertie too, which she loved. Our friendship strengthened no end and I'm actually really grateful to Covid for this. However, I realised I was worried about her, and was aware this added further stress to my already strained nerves.

The third lockdown ended after fourteen weeks. Finally. This isolation was the longest so far. It was a little better than the previous two, with being able to see Lucy and Sasha, and also to help Amy, but it still seemed never-ending and I missed my family desperately.

The months ticked on. The UK rescinded its strict rules bit by bit, particularly as the vaccination programme picked up speed. I decided to get a friend for Bertie. I felt bad that I'd leave him lonely while I worked so many shifts. Bertie's litter sister had had kits, so little Mabel came home with me in June.

The stresses of this last lockdown seemed to accumulate on top of the previous two. I was left feeling the most frustrated, lonely and tearful I had ever been. I still struggled to drop off to sleep, my eating habits weren't good and my days off were largely spent in solitude. As 2021 progressed, my stress levels just seemed to mount. My house purchase was delayed over and over due to yet more complications with the leasehold of the flat. My grandad was poorly and in and out of hospital a lot. This worried my mum so I was concerned for her too, but being a distance away meant I was helpless when it came to doing anything. I was still supporting Amy and that was a worry in its own way. I also felt I was a bit of a burden to my new watch, who were still trying to get to know me and were amazingly supportive, but I knew I was withdrawn and not really myself.

I knew too that I could feel myself reaching the end of my tether; I sensed I may break as soon as I moved house. I couldn't cope with much more.

CHAPTER 7
PTSD

Everything changed for me the night of 17th August, 2021. I was working an overtime shift with Green Watch. Looking back, I can see I'd been feeling wobbly all week; the fifth anniversary of the A34 crash had passed just a few days previously and was very much at the forefront of my mind. I was also becoming increasingly agitated about the house move that should already have happened. Various other things seemed to weigh down on me too. It all meant I was scrabbling to maintain some form of stability in my head. Work, as always, was a distraction for me and kept my thoughts busy. On this night though, this was to my detriment.

Just before 22:00hrs, the 9s lit up. Several calls were received regarding a car hitting a bridge and bursting into flames. Later calls stated that persons were still within the vehicle, which was now well alight. I was positioned on primary radio that night, so I contacted the crews en route to inform them of the details. One crew wasn't answering my calls, which made me jittery. As a con-op, you develop a sense for whether a call is going to end up being a serious incident or not – quite often it turns out to be a lot less scary than the picture panicked callers can portray. But instinct was screaming at me that this job was not going to be a good one. The first crew in attendance were informed in plenty of time, however, so I knew no firefighters would be walking into the situation blind. The first impressions message came across the radio that the car was indeed well alight; the second message, just five minutes later, described an unknown number of fatalities in the vehicle.

My whole body went cold. I fought to remain in control of myself, aware of strange physical reactions I'd never really experienced before within my working career. Adrenaline coursed through my body and I was trembling; my heart was pounding out of my chest. I was nauseous and, despite feeling icy within, my hands were sweating. I suppressed and pushed what I was feeling aside; I needed to stay in the game and I desperately wanted to know more.

There were three occupants confirmed to be in that vehicle. I managed to remain in my seat for approximately an hour, ignoring my squirming insides and my desperate need to run away, and try to focus on the job at hand. At an appropriate time, I eventually excused myself from the control room to go to the toilets. As I stood up to leave the room, I caught Clara's eye. Clara was the crew manager on duty that night; we'd been friends for many years and something in my expression must have told her I wasn't right. I made it to the bathroom shortly before dissolving into tears. Clara walked in only a few minutes later to find me shaking and crying over the sinks, not knowing what to do with myself. She hugged me – neither of us are huggers so this was a sign something was truly wrong! Then we talked.

This was a very out-of-character reaction for me. I'm someone who has always prided myself on the ability to deal with incidents with a sense of personal detachment, keeping work out of my own head. I explained to her that I was probably just feeling overly emotional because of the anniversary of the earlier crash on 10th August. As I said it, I realised I was connecting the two incidents and joining the dots. Here, again, was an entire car full of young people with their whole lives ahead of them, wiped out in a single moment. And I was helpless to do anything for them.

Clara remained with me for several more minutes until I'd pulled myself together a little. I wanted to see the job through to the end but was due to take my break first. So, when she returned to the control room a little later, Clara arranged it so another con-op would swap breaks with me. Then so could sit it through. I knew there was no more to be done; that nothing I could do would change the outcome. But something in me wanted – needed – to see the job out in its entirety.

I remember remaining subdued for the rest of that shift. A further call, at my request, to an officer on scene was made by Clara to find out more details, and it was established that these were teenagers likely driving too fast and ultimately losing control. My brain couldn't stop going over and over it; terrible thoughts of both this incident and the previous one. I felt almost numb; exhausted and fluey from the come down after the huge adrenaline spike I'd experienced. I was shattered.

As handover for the oncoming shift approached, Keith, our group manager, appeared in the doorway. I believe the day shift was short of staff – Covid was doing the rounds, hence my requirement on overtime too – so Keith, ordinarily based in his office over the corridor, was covering the shift himself to keep numbers up. He looked at me strangely as he stood at the front of the room and chatted to us all. When I finally got up to leave and passed him at the door, he asked me if I was feeling ok. My brain was totally scrambled by then. I replied to him with a flippant comment – something about it always being me who ended up killing cars full of kids. I bid him goodbye and headed off to my car.

Three things happened over the next few days. First, it was like a dam had burst in my mind. I found myself following the media coverage about this most recent crash to find out everything I could about the teens who had died. But I also found myself looking at older media reports about the 2016 A34 crash. Very soon, the older job had completely taken over my mind, far more than the most recent one. Over the next few days, things escalated. Sleep became erratic; nightmares started again; and the banging of cars colliding would jolt me out of sleep frequently. I also became very tearful – more so than the usual isolation crying that had become a new normal for me. I was more impatient and irritable with everything around me too.

Secondly, I received a message from Malcolm the next afternoon after the crash. Malcolm was the watch manager in charge of the overtime shift I had worked, and he informed me that trauma support had been arranged for us the following week. This is something that has become more routine in recent years, and I was grateful it had been scheduled so promptly. I don't remember requesting it so my managers must have sorted it on my behalf.

Trauma support happened on 23rd August, and I was surprised to note that I was the only person from that shift who'd been referred. In my mind, I was expecting all of us from that night to be there. Malcolm attended too, as some moral support for me, and I was relieved to discover the volunteer conducting the support was actually someone I knew through instructing fire cadets. She was very approachable and we discussed the incident and my reaction to it, and how I was feeling now. To my mortification, I ended up bursting into tears. Despite all the crying I'd done during the pandemic, the majority of it had been in private, so to explode in front of someone like that was not something I expected at all. The volunteer was very good – and poor Malcolm tried to be supportive but had no idea what to do with me or where to look. I wasn't someone who just openly wept on my colleagues. She suggested this latest incident seemed to have triggered my emotions from the earlier A34 RTC, and believed I should talk to my GP or approach Talking Therapies offered on the NHS. I refused these options – I wasn't ill – so she proposed seeing me in a fortnight's time, when quite often initial trauma reactions start to subside. I agreed to this.

Thirdly, when back in on shift the following week, I was called into Keith's office to talk. He told me, very calmly but full of concern, that he believed he recognised my reaction to my last shift as symptoms of Post-Traumatic Stress Disorder. Specifically, my comment to him as I left – alongside my whole demeanour generally – seemed very out of character to him. I think he had also discretely enquired about me with a couple of colleagues to gauge how I'd been recently. (In later months, we were to discuss this initial interaction, and he told me he'd also done some research into the A34 crash, to understand more of the full picture before approaching me.)

Keith had obviously dwelt on my reaction a lot over those few days, and felt it serious enough to approach me as soon as he did. He strongly encouraged me to speak to a professional and get some help. This seemed a complete overreaction to me and took me by surprise. It seemed such a trivial thing to ring people about, and such a waste of time. Just one bad job? One off shift? I'd never had physical reactions to my work before and I put my emotional response down to already being vulnerable and wobbly due to the pandemic. But the severity of Keith's tone and the fact he was actually having this discussion with me – as a group manager with experience of having seen PTSD in others – made me think hard. He explained that even a one-off reaction proved something deeper was going on and needed to be addressed, as it wouldn't go away on its own. I was clearly burying something that needed to be sorted.

We discussed options for who I could ring; I wasn't

keen initially on speaking to my GP as that made it very serious. I didn't feel it warranted that after one blip. I was also terrified, with it being a trauma related to a car crash, that they'd tell me to stop driving. I knew my driving capabilities were fine and that I was safe; I knew better than most people the consequences of not being in a fit position to drive a vehicle and I'd never allow that to happen. Thankfully, there seemed to be other routes to go down within the brigade first – namely with our Employee Assistance Programme (EAP) and through a contract with a medical company. I promised Keith I'd consider making a phone call and would think about what he'd said – but I wanted to finish attending the trauma support sessions first before reaching out.

The second trauma support session on 5th September was a fairly swift meeting. I was touched that the volunteer had travelled into work on a Sunday to catch me when I was next on duty. But it was clear to both of us by now that things were perhaps a little more severe than our meetings would be able to fix. The car fire a couple of weeks ago had now faded into the back of my memory, as other jobs did, and no longer bothered me. The A34 incident, however, was extremely prominent and wouldn't let up in my mind. It was the first time I'd ever really talked about it and every time I did, my body – particularly my hands – would visibly shake. Speaking about it twice in these trauma sessions, and talking to Keith too, was bringing out symptoms I had no idea my body had been hiding for so long. We agreed that perhaps the time had come to ask for some extra help.

I had further discussions with Keith, and chats with

Sam (my station manager) and Debbie (my watch manager) after he had also informed them. All three talked me through my options patiently, until I finally came to accept that ringing an agency to ask for help was the next stage in the process. The chats with both Keith and Sam especially were convincing and concerning to me. I was quite happy to talk to them, but as they had both joined the brigade in recent years and weren't my managers when the initial crash took place, I found myself having to retell the story again and again. I didn't go into detail; I glossed over with a broad description of what happened. But I discovered that every time I mentioned it, or actively thought about it, my physical symptoms became more pronounced, in particular my shaking hands and heart palpitations. It was this somatic response, and their solemn, patient tones as they allowed my mind time to convince itself this was actually a real thing to be addressed, that gave me the push I needed to reach out for further help.

I eventually plucked up the courage to contact the EAP on 8th September. I did so when on shift as I knew Debbie wouldn't let me back out of it. They were surprisingly difficult to get hold of – I rang them at the beginning of my shift at 18:00hrs and was told to expect a phone call back within a set time frame. After chasing several times, I finally got a call back at midnight. The lady I spoke to was sympathetic but advised that my case sounded too complicated for them to be able to deal with – their limited capacity of providing six sessions of counselling would only leave me more vulnerable. She advised me to contact my GP instead. I came away from that phone call shaky, disheartened and rather daunted; after taking so long to psyche myself up to get in contact, I was being told I was a tricky case and they couldn't help me. I wasn't expecting that.

I rang the other helpline available through work, the private medical provider, when back in Control a few days afterwards. They said something very similar: that I sounded too severe for them to deal with and they recommended I contact my doctor. They went one step further, though: they would send a letter to my GP detailing our conversation. I was told to give it a couple of days, then ring my surgery for an appointment. This terrified me. However, with other avenues now closed, it seemed to be the only option.

I rang my GP surgery on the 15th September. Appointments were scarce, I knew, and filtered heavily by reception due to still being in a pandemic. I was surprised therefore to have an almost immediate call back from the doctor. I ran through the whole situation again: the initial A34 crash; the most recent call and my reaction; my manager suspecting PTSD and this being echoed by the trauma support team, EAP and the medical company. By the time I'd finished, I was trembling violently and felt sick.

The doctor advised I should speak to Talking Therapies, who deal with mental health issues and would triage me for appropriate treatment/therapy. He advised that going sick might not be a bad thing. I explained my home situation and that I didn't want any time off work if I could avoid it. But I was torn; work was now becoming a double-edged sword, both my safe space and a danger zone rolled into one. I knew I wanted to keep working, at least until I'd moved house and had more support and stability around me. The doctor agreed that was a sensible course of action and told me to remain registered with my current medical practice around the house move, to keep some consistency to my mental health referral. I rang Talking Therapies immediately afterwards so I wouldn't bottle it. They asked more questions, and I was given a forty-minute telephone appointment for the following week, on 22nd September.

By this point, my physical symptoms were starting to take over whenever I was at work. I felt extreme jolts of adrenaline shooting through my body; I would visibly shake and I could feel palpitations and nausea on and off throughout my shift, which I attributed to those shocks. It didn't take me long to put two and two together – I seemed to react strongly whenever we received calls to an RTC. Our control room covered three counties so I was trying to handle several collisions every shift. My ears would prick up each time a call of that nature came in and my anxiety would hit the roof. The symptoms seemed to become more pronounced after I'd spoken to my GP and then to Talking Therapies. It was as if my brain had lost just a little more control over something I'd held tightly at bay for five years now.

But as I seemed to worsen, I also noted that I had incredible, extraordinary friends. Clara had messaged me several times since being on shift together for the car fire; checking in on me and supporting me as things progressed. She worked on Greens with Richard, another good friend, who was my crew manager when back on White Watch. We'd crossed paths briefly straight after my meeting with Keith, when I was reeling from his opinion that I could have PTSD. Richard and I hadn't had a chance to chat directly then, due to having headquarters staff around us, but he knew I wasn't right and messaged me later that day. He, too, then continued to check in and support me. I also talked through everything with Sasha and Lucy; they were my only civilian friends not in the job who seemed to understand, and were amazingly supportive too. I felt very loved, and humbled that, at the beginning of my journey, I already had people rallying around me.

The 22nd September arrived and Sasha very kindly offered to be with me for the duration of my phone call appointment. A Talking Therapies counsellor ran through a lot of questions, thoroughly assessing the severity of my symptoms to decide on the right course of action. She asked about low mood (PHQ-9) and levels of anxiety (GAD-7), explaining that it was common for people with PTSD to have some symptoms of depression and to feel anxious as part of the condition. I felt like a bit of a fraud still – it all seemed very serious, particularly when she asked if I had any thoughts of self-harm or suicide. I almost didn't feel my case was valid enough to warrant her time. Fortunately, I didn't feel suicidal, although to their credit, every official person I'd spoken to had asked that question and signposted me to emergency help for if I ever felt I was in crisis.

I was completely shocked when the counsellor read out my scores at the end of those brief assessments – declaring that both my low mood and anxiety levels were rated as severe. My specific trauma score, measured by something called a PCL-5, was rated out of eighty. Scores of over thirty indicated PTSD and that trauma therapy would be beneficial; I scored forty-three on that first assessment. I also noted, when explaining my situation, that at one point the counsellor became completely lost for words. I didn't think that could be a good sign! She told me she would liaise with her supervisor and get back to me regarding treatment in a few days. It later transpired that, after conversations between herself and her supervisor, they'd decided to escalate me to their senior team. In her words, I was a "complicated case" – a description that seemed to be echoed back to me several times over the course of the following few months. She suspected that Cognitive Behavioural Therapy would be the best course of action, but I was to wait and be assessed further.

The following day, I had a catch-up meeting with Keith to explain the steps I'd taken so far. I told him the doctor wanted to sign me off sick, but had accepted my reasoning as to why I felt I needed to remain in work. I was also very aware that I didn't want to develop a phobia of being in the control room or dealing with RTCs. The way to combat that, I felt, was to continue to immerse myself in my role. Keith was very understanding about it all. He seemed rather shocked that the whole time I was talking to him, my hands were trembling uncontrollably. This was a marked change from just a couple of weeks ago when we'd had that initial talk together. He mentioned that Richard had been in to chat too, concerned about me. I could barely keep up with how quickly I seemed to be declining and the rate at which my symptoms were progressing, so it was a relief to know they were both there. Almost like having a safety net.

Keith told me to do what I needed to do – he was happy for me to book sick when it felt appropriate, but it was also no problem for me to stay in work, or indeed to cancel my upcoming leave if I felt I couldn't deal with prolonged time off. I asked to temporarily adjust my role a little; I'd realised by now that taking 999 calls had a harsher effect on me than dealing with radio messages. The stress of talking to members of the public about a collision tended to send shockwaves through my whole being. Keith was incredibly accommodating and removed me from 9s calls for as long as was necessary. At least, I didn't have to sit in the 9s positions for the foreseeable shifts and could stick to radio and admin calls. Should the 9s be ringing, however, when my colleagues were already busy, I was still willing to jump in and help. Keith also encouraged me to use the gym facilities in the building whenever was needed, to combat the excess adrenaline that was coursing around my blood and causing me to shake.

I came out of that chat feeling very grateful, although slightly overwhelmed at how big this had blown up to be in just a matter of weeks.

I updated Debbie too, as she was my watch manager. She agreed with all that had been discussed and was happy to keep me to radio and admin roles for the time being. I also explained the situation to a few others, including my crew manager, Marcus and a fellow con-op, Harriet. Debbie made sure that either she, Marcus or Harriet were always in the room with me, so if I reacted, there was support there. I felt guilty for not informing rest of the watch. They knew something was up because of my behaviour, the various meetings out of the room, and now the announcement that my role was to be altered slightly and I was to be with certain people when breaks were chosen. But everybody seemed to take it in their stride without complaint or questioning me. I knew I'd have to tell them eventually – especially as this wasn't going to resolve itself overnight – but I was still wrapping my head around it and every time I spoke about it to someone new, I seemed to have a worsening reaction. So I stayed quiet for as long as I needed, and was incredibly grateful to those I'd confided in, who also kept it confidential.

Finally – *finally* – moving day came. My house purchase and flat sale completed on 15th October, 2021. After a stressful lead-up and a tense day of waiting to complete before the movers could go ahead, I was in my new house at last by that evening. Instantly, I felt a million times better. The suffocating loneliness cloud suddenly lifted. I hadn't lived in my hometown for seven years, but it still felt as familiar as ever. The house, rundown as it was and desperately needing attention, felt lived in and homely.

I spent that night christening my new home with pizza and wine, with my friend Georgia – and in the following days caught up with four old friends, my parents and my brother. I also had a doorstep visit from the daughter of the previous house owner, gifting me flowers and wishing me well. The bunnies were looked after by Lucy for the day of the move, and she drove them back to me the following day. Even being able to do that – to show someone around my new home – was a world apart from my last moving day and felt incredibly uplifting. The rabbits settled into their own room and loved the window sill they could sit upon to watch the world go by. Slowly, I set about sorting through boxes and making the place my own.

My next appointment – with a member of the senior team from Talking Therapies this time – took place via video call a week later on 21st October, a month on from my previous assessment. He was a CBT practitioner and I believe was assessing my suitability for this type of therapy. He also ran through the standard PHQ-9, GAD-7 and PCL-5 questions and recorded the new score. He confirmed that I had Single Incident PTSD, which was a delayed onset brought out via the pandemic and various other stressors. The practitioner described it to me as memories being stored incorrectly in my brain. My brain was behaving as though I was constantly under threat, with my working shifts being spent in fight-or-flight mode. At the end of the call, he advised that he believed one-to-one Trauma-Focused CBT would be the most beneficial, but he had to confer with his supervisors before actioning this.

I was relieved that finally a plan seemed to be coming together. However, I was a little concerned about the number of supervisors being liaised with throughout my assessments. Exactly how broken was I?! I was also a little proud, in a strange way, to think that I had staved off PTSD for five years and that it took a global pandemic to finally break me. It was bizarre to realise how much I'd been burying and trying to manage as time moved on. Now, with my house move finally complete and therapy in the not-too-distant future, things were looking hopeful.

CHAPTER 8
IN LIMBO

The next weeks fully proved to me how much I had masked and buried my PTSD. I'd blamed a lot of my symptoms on being lonely and isolated, but that particular problem had seemingly been solved overnight with my house move. So now, I was left with pure trauma to deal with. My body took over.

My reactions at work, initially something I felt I could hide from my colleagues, became quite severe and very obvious as time went on. Often jobs – nearly always RTCs – would have my brain screaming at me to leave the room; to run from the situation. My nerves, all my instincts shouted that I was in danger and needed to escape. I would end up leaving the control room and retreating to the balcony of our headquarters building, craving cold, fresh air and feeling rather claustrophobic. Massive amounts of adrenaline would be coursing through my bloodstream. I'd have palpitations, sweating, nausea; I'd often cry uncontrollably. My breathing would be erratic and my shaking intense. It wasn't just my hands – my whole being trembled violently. My body seemed to go into a fearful, protective mode: I couldn't meet anybody's eyes, I struggled to string sentences together, and I couldn't stand to be touched by most people until all this started to reduce and the adrenaline ebbed away. This, I supposed, was my brain kicking into flight mode.

My colleagues were amazing; they picked up very quickly that the best approach was to ignore me, leave me to gather my senses, then talk to me when I was able to verbalise again. Hugs were always welcome on the come-down; the sudden rush and then dispersal of adrenaline often made me feel weak and fluey afterwards. It was strange to note, though, that my reactions were predominantly physical – I didn't notice particular emotions when I was triggered, only frustrations with myself afterwards for acting in a way I felt was irrational. The adrenaline and heart palpitations made me feel panicked but otherwise everything seemed to be somatic.

Gradually, I told all members of my watch what was going on; a few people at a time, to avoid it feeling like a formal announcement. I could no longer hide my blatant reactions and they deserved to know the truth after supporting me blindly for so long. This was very hard for me; it seemed the more I told people and talked about it, the more pronounced it became. I was also still trying to understand it myself. I'd never really had to lean on other people for support before; I'd always prided myself on being self-sufficient and able to stand on my own two feet. Yet this whole process was making me learn that I *had* to rely on a few individuals at least. I couldn't get through this alone and needed friends to support me, both when I was triggered and while navigating the help being offered. A couple of watch members were on restricted or reduced hours at the time and I didn't tell them straight away: baby steps, I guess. They were dealing with their own issues and crossed paths with me less frequently. As they rejoined the workplace more fully, I then spoke to them too. I also asked my watch not to talk to the rest of Control; I still wasn't comfortable with it being common knowledge. They kept their word and I was humbled to be able to trust them so fully.

So, work continued to be both a safe space and a danger zone. I relied on my colleagues for moral support, as PTSD wasn't something I was yet ready to discuss with family or many of my civilian friends. I'd mentioned it to Beth and Georgia, testing the waters. They tried to listen but didn't really know what to say, and tended to avoid the conversation afterwards. It clearly made them both uncomfortable so I stopped trying to talk about it. My friends Sasha and Lucy, of course, were the exceptions to the rule and were both fabulous. I also kept Joseph informed. He was a good friend from JCs and cadets and, historically, someone I would always run to for a cuppa and a natter when things got tough. It worked both ways and I'd been a strength for him too on various occasions in the years before. However, our friendship changed a lot when the pandemic hit; his role shifted to working from home rather than being based at fire stations, and he conducted many house visits as his workload altered. His mindset was also reaching for retirement and, with both of our changing circumstances, we didn't get many opportunities to chat the way we once had. I kept him informed of my journey, but it was difficult when he didn't seem to understand or acknowledge the severity of it – or at least, if he did, he didn't seem to appreciate that now was the time I needed his friendship the most, rather than it dwindling down the way it seemed to be doing. But again, I accepted that his experience of the pandemic was very different to mine. He was living close to all his family and his job meant still coming into contact with various people every day. Without seeing me in person, I don't think the full extent of my distress really sank in.

I felt I was now in a kind of limbo state. I continued to work as much as I could, in the best way I could, trying to fend off reactions and hoping that each next call would be less triggering. I was able to withstand it if I had to take a call; I pushed down my reaction and suppressed any internal screaming to get up and run, remaining professional until that conversation was over. Then my brain would catch up and explode into complete flight mode and I'd have to leave the room.

I was also now struggling with a particular part of my journey into work: my commute from my new house meant once again travelling past the crash site twice a day. Again, I was able to keep my head straight and force down any reactions, the way I did if I had to take a 9s call at work, remaining in safe control of the vehicle. I was ultra aware of what happens when you're not in control of a car on the road and I would never insist on driving if I wasn't up to it. Seeing that specific stretch of carriageway now always reduced me to tears, but I refused to reroute my journey for fear of developing a phobia of that particular area. I wouldn't back down and let PTSD control which way I drove, even if it meant crying every time I took that route.

I was discovering hypervigilance – I was acutely aware of every other road user around me. This, if anything, made me a better driver than ever before. However, swallowing my body's reactions until it was safe to let go meant I would quite often become a shaky mess at the end of my journey, once I'd parked the car and allowed my thoughts to catch up. Still, my stubborn streak prevailed: I refused to back down and go sick from work, and I refused to change my route to work. I believe this stubborn trait actually held me in good stead for the long journey of recovery this was about to become.

I had to wait to hear that my first CBT appointment had been approved and arranged. Until that happened, it was a case of managing day to day. At the beginning of November, I contacted the Fire Fighters Charity at the suggestion of colleagues. The charity provides help to fire service employees in the form of both physical and mental rehabilitation, and they have three centres across the UK to help facilitate this. I was hesitant to reach out to yet another organisation for fear of being rebutted again. But I needn't have worried; the charity staff were fantastic. The lady I liaised with offered me two options: I could go and use their facilities for a respite week – a few days away to relax and recharge; or I could attend a reset week, in which I would be part of scheduled activities including hiking and gym sessions, mindfulness and yoga classes. I would also attend classroom sessions based on things like nutrition, sleep hygiene and dealing with stress. The latter option sounded ideal for me, so I booked myself on to the next course running at the end of the month. I had to fill in an application form so they knew what was bringing me to them; writing even a brief summary of events made me shaky and tearful. I also had to have assessments over the phone for my physical abilities and dietary needs. It was made clear to me that, although they offered other sources of help in the form of counselling, they wouldn't delve into this with me as I was awaiting formal CBT treatment. They didn't want their counselling to conflict with that. I agreed, and looked forward to a break away after so long.

The 17th November threw me a curveball. I was on the primary radio position when a priority message flashed across the screen. I took the radio to hear that an officer had come across a running call, meaning he'd discovered an emergency situation when out and about. This was an RTC with a family, including a baby, in the car. My reaction was dramatic and immediate – it was like the car fire in August all over again. It hit me like a bolt of lightning. I forced my brain to carry out the actions I needed to take immediately: type the message out, find the address and create the incident, then mobilise crews and inform them of the nature of the call. Then I stood up and left the room, feeling as though the world around me was a bit of a blur and trying not to explode as I allowed my suppressed reaction to finally take over.

I made it out onto the balcony, a shaky, tearful mess, full of adrenaline and heart palpitations and feeling a bit like a rabbit caught in headlights, with my senses on overdrive. Keith was sitting on a chair in the corner of the balcony. He'd been in the control room when the priority message had come in, had seen my instant change in demeanour and headed to the balcony. He knew that's where I'd scarper to. He could see how much my body was reacting physically and suggested we go for a walk. My brain was scrambled and I couldn't say much but I agreed. I walked with him at a brisk pace out of the building, up the road and around the industrial estate, trying to burn off the copious amounts of adrenaline, calm my fear reaction and restore my body to normal. It was the worst trigger I'd experienced since the car fire that had seemed to precipitate this series of events. I believe it was both because a child was involved and I'd been caught unawares: the officer who called it in radioed out of nowhere, not being attached to any job, and caught me completely off guard.

The comedown from that massive reaction was huge. I was pale, nauseous and felt weak and fluey for the rest of the day. Keith and Sam kept "popping in" to speak to us in the control room for various reasons throughout the shift, but I knew this was a pretence to check on me. I think I scared them a bit that day. When I eventually headed home to bed, I was absolutely drained.

The next day I was better but still not right. I was grateful that Keith allowed me to manage it in my own way without feeling under pressure to go off sick. Others were starting to advise that perhaps a break away from the workplace would be best. Clara quite rightly pointed out that most people would have booked off work by now, and that giving myself a rest might be the wisest course of action. Debbie was of a similar opinion and, after discussions, I made an agreement with her: I was holding out for my first CBT session and my trip to the Fire Fighters Charity – I would reassess after that and see what I needed to do. Despite receiving a shot of adrenaline every time the 9s line rang in the room, despite having palpitations on and off for the duration of each shift, despite being triggered when the RTC calls did come in – I still did not want to book sick. I didn't want to give in to this; I didn't want to cease momentum and I feared what would happen when I did. I didn't want to become fearful of even setting foot in my workplace. And I didn't want to isolate myself when most of my support through this PTSD journey was through my colleagues. I knew I couldn't handle any more loneliness and didn't want to cut myself off physically from my support network.

So, I continued in limbo.

CHAPTER 9
HARCOMBE HOUSE

My first Trauma-Focused Cognitive Behavioural Therapy session was on 22nd November 2021. It was a video call appointment, as they were all to be due to Covid. It felt almost underwhelming after waiting for so long. Much of it was introductory content, explaining how the sessions would be laid out and asking me why I was referred. I was surprised to learn I'd been allocated twenty sessions' worth of therapy. I'd been of the understanding that eight or twelve sessions was the norm. Twenty weeks would lead me into April, which seemed like forever away. I asked Therapist Lady – as she became known in my head – her opinion on my booking sick. She was rather non-committal, saying there were pros and cons to both staying in work and taking some time out.

Due to this first session only being formalities, and with my upcoming trip to the Fire Fighters Charity scheduled for the following week, my next session was booked just a few days later, for the 26th. This hour was a lot more productive. Therapist Lady explained the wardrobe analogy to me – how certain traumatic memories are not processed properly and, while in survival mode, the brain stores them incorrectly. This is akin to shoving a duvet full of stinging nettles into a wardrobe and forcing it closed. Eventually, after trying to keep it shut for so long, it will burst open. The duvet – or memory – needs to be organised properly and folded away as it should be onto the right shelf, despite it being painful when handled. That all seemed to make sense to me. We discussed grounding techniques to bring myself back under control more quickly when I found myself being triggered. I was a bit sceptical of this – it sounded rather wishy-washy to me – but I was willing to give anything a try.

Therapist Lady informed me that I had delayed-onset PTSD and explained how that had come about: the changes in all my circumstances, my stress and the isolation I felt during the pandemic basically meant my usual mental resilience and coping mechanisms had failed. Old trauma rose back up with a vengeance; Covid-19 was ultimately my undoing. I did wonder what would have happened if the coronavirus hadn't come about. How long would I have continued with PTSD buried beneath the surface? I was tasked with homework – to practise grounding techniques – which I agreed to try but discovered it was something I wrestled with: if I practised when not triggered, I found intrusive thoughts consumed me. But trying to ground myself when I *was* triggered seemed pointless, as my brain and body took over in some kind of primal flight reaction. I often struggled even to talk; there was no way I could focus on other distraction techniques.

Two days later, I was packing my bags and heading to the Fire Fighters Charity. I would be based at Harcombe House in Devon, a beautiful manor set in idyllic grounds and the ultimate recuperation venue. I handed bunny-sitting responsibilities to my sister and wove my way down south through counties dusted with snow. I told a bit of a white lie to my family – they still had no idea about my PTSD so I was unsure how to mention this trip. I said we'd been offered the chance to go on a reset week after working through the pandemic, which technically was true. No questions were really asked and this seemed to be a plausible reason in their eyes for a free holiday to Devon. I felt guilty not telling them the whole truth but I just couldn't bring myself to do it yet.

I arrived at Harcombe House mid-afternoon on the Sunday as instructed, settled into my room, and had a quick look round the site before dinner was scheduled. It was truly a stunning place, the grounds boasting a water feature surrounded by a perfectly tended garden, which was colourful and vibrant even in the wintry November. Dinner was delicious, set in a dining room with tables well spaced out to take Covid restrictions into consideration. It was a strange time, the centre once again open for business following the pandemic, but with people still being cautious. There only seemed to be one course running at a time because of this, so it became quickly evident who I'd be spending time with by who showed up for food. There were only eight of us in total, a perfect number, I felt, and we chatted over our meal, getting to know each other. We were all there for a variety of reasons and from different brigades; from differing positions within the service too.

After the meal, it was agreed a few of us would head to the bar on site to continue the chat we'd started. I ended up going for a drink with two others, one from Derbyshire and a retired firefighter from my own county. Comparing our backgrounds went fine – until the retired firefighter addressed me and asked: "You're in Control. Do you remember this job on…?"

I felt the blood drain from my face when I forced myself to answer him that yes, I remembered that incident; that it had actually caused me to develop PTSD, which was why I was at the charity today.

I couldn't believe my bad luck. Of all the people I could have met and all the conversations we could have had, I'd managed to fall into that particular chat before my week had even started! The man was very apologetic, and both he and the other person with us insisted I didn't have to talk about it if I wasn't comfortable. They were so kind.

But after all, wasn't that why I was there? Wasn't talking a part of it all? So I told them, rather broadly, what my story was. My voice cracked and my hands shook as I did so. However, it acted as an ice-breaker. Both of them then opened up about their own mental health struggles that had brought them to Harcombe House. We ended up having a rather frank, honest conversation over our couple of pints of cider. It was emotional, but bonding, and I felt it started us on a good footing for the week ahead.

The next morning, we all saw our timetable, which

was pretty full-on for the few days to come. That Monday included some classroom sessions, with a sleep workshop and "goals group" – what we wanted to get out of this experience and how to go about things moving forward. We also had more practical sessions slotted in between, including time in the gym, a walk and then an evening's instruction in Tai Chi.

I found the goals group rather tough. The instructor leading the workshop asked each of us what our aims were. For me, that was an inordinately huge question. I wanted to feel like me again; the old me, before PTSD and before Covid. I wanted to learn how to cope with being triggered; how to keep my head tethered rather than the whole world spiralling whenever an RTC cropped up. I wanted to eat properly and to sleep well. I wanted to stop crying most days. I wanted the nightmares to stop, the unwelcome thoughts to stop dominating my brain, the sense of panic and doom to stop following me. I wanted to no longer be a burden to my work friends, and to hold myself at less of an emotional distance from my family. I wanted to feel less isolated – somehow, although I was now surrounded by loved ones and living in a familiar town, there was still something huge separating me from the rest of the world. I wanted to feel in control of myself again.

I was under no illusions that a five-day respite would be able to fix any of that. But I considered that a reasonable goal would be to learn some coping strategies, particularly to help me at work. To explain that, I had to give some form of context to the room. I ended up launching again into what I'd told my two new friends the night before in the bar. This time, I cried: big, ugly crying that I couldn't seem to stem. I should have felt mortified at sobbing in front of complete strangers, but somehow I didn't care. They didn't either; in truth, some of them also got a little tearful, and certainly opened up themselves. I was realising just how powerful talking was.

Through the hike later in the day, the conversation that had been started in the classroom seemed to continue. I walked with a firefighter from Surrey, who could resonate with my experiences through some of his own. We talked deeply for most of the hike, the cold air refreshing me and clearing my head a little. He seemed to be the one person in the group who "got it", having suffered trauma himself.

The rest of the day was good but perhaps missed the mark a little for what I needed at the time. Although the sleep workshop was informative and my group seemed to take a lot from it, I already knew what good sleep hygiene was. I'd always been a good sleeper up until recent events. My PTSD symptoms were the problem: intrusive thoughts, a constantly whirring mind and ridiculous amounts of adrenaline prevented me from falling asleep; nightmares and hearing cars crashing, causing me to jolt awake in the middle of the night, were what made me struggle to stay asleep.

I felt the same about the gym session – it was great for a lot of my group. Programmes were individually tailored for group members with specific injuries or disabilities; but for me, I struggled with the energy or inclination to even leave the house on a day-to-day basis. I participated in every gym session at Harcombe, but I knew I didn't have the mental capacity to continue that momentum once I returned home.

The following days continued in much the same way. It was an incredibly well-run, thought-out programme, and a good break in what my life had recently become. Personally, though, I didn't find it quite specific enough. I got the most out of talking to others who could relate to my experience, and picked bits out of the workshops that were applicable. I loved the hikes. We did a mindfulness walk, which made me realise that, although I wasn't in a very tolerant position to be focusing on mindful thinking, I was already automatically using fresh, cold air to clear my thoughts; that in itself was a form of grounding. It tied in with my actions at work: I would crave the outdoor space of the balcony instinctively when triggered, in much the same way.

We also had a nutrition workshop along the same lines as the sleep workshop; helpful, but not applicable necessarily to at that time. I wasn't very good at the Tai Chi or yoga – I'm clumsy, physically inflexible, and impatient. I ended up just giggling at my own lopsided efforts to move as I should, but I enjoyed the tutorials all the same.

The most beneficial sessions for me were the "Understanding Stress" and "Loss and Change" workshops – here, at last, I could relate to much of what was being discussed. I stopped to talk to the instructor after the stress workshop, to chat and probe further, and ended up missing the swimming session directly afterwards to continue talking to her. I picked her brains a little about my own situation; she was very patient with my ramblings and my getting upset yet again. Her insight was that I was fearful of booking myself off sick, after having fought to not be at home on my own for so long throughout the pandemic. She advised that I should listen to my body because clearly my illness was coming out in somatic symptoms – my brain was still refusing to catch up and was trying to bury everything and block out the stress I was feeling. If my reactions were getting worse at work, then I shouldn't ignore that. She gave me a lot of food for thought.

The chats where everyone fed back after each session were fabulous too, as were the bar meets in the evening. The latter were less about drinking and more about communicating, relating to each other and reflecting on the day. I finished the week grateful for everyone I'd met and shared with, and feeling so fortunate to have been able to use the facilities for a whole five days. But although I'd got a lot out of my stay, I now dreaded heading home back into my PTSD hell, away from this safer bubble that had been created so briefly.

CHAPTER 10
SPIRALLING

My drive home from Devon scared me a little. Not the actual journey or the other road users but my own inner self; my thoughts, and the feelings now churning inside me. I felt extremely shaken and anxious, probably because of what I was returning to. Harcombe had taught me a lot and I'd met new friends I vowed to stay in contact with. Yet the reality was that I'd just spent five days pouring my heart out and telling complete strangers about the life I was still trying to wrap my head around. I'd cried a lot over the last few days and felt very vulnerable. It seemed to me I'd lifted a lid off of something my brain had subconsciously been trying to keep sealed in. And now what? I was to return to my house, to my job; to try to continue my life while PTSD raged, only this time I seemed to have dented my defences to fight it.

The following day I was back at work. It was a

fairly uneventful shift, although my heart continued to jump every time the 9s rang. I was utterly exhausted – from a full-on week at the charity, from a poor night's sleep yet again, and from the little jolts of adrenaline fed to me throughout the day. I found myself napping on my hour's lunch break, curled up in an armchair in the restroom; not something I'd ever done before but I couldn't stop my eyes from closing. My colleagues humoured me and left me alone to snooze for a bit.

I was scheduled to attend our work's Christmas party that evening. I'd agreed to go along for the meal – in a Latino restaurant with live music – but would stick to soft drinks so I could drive home when they inevitably moved on to a bar afterwards. I knew I'd be exhausted from a busy few days in Devon, but I wasn't prepared to feel quite as emotionally wiped out as I was. One friend on my watch, Daniel, seemed to be paying close attention to me. He'd been to Harcombe House on a previous occasion and had messaged me a couple of times during my stay to check in. He could tell this work night out was the last thing I needed. We ended up sitting together during the meal, which was tapas-style food. The dinner was delicious, but I didn't seem to have a huge appetite. I was also very on edge and became increasingly jumpy as the evening went on, although I couldn't put my finger on why. My hands trembled the whole time and I withdrew more and more. I remained in my seat for the sake of it being our Christmas meal, but actually I just wanted to retreat home to my bed. In hindsight, it's obvious why I became so affected: the live music was banging and noisy, with the band placed right beside our table. My tolerance for loud noises these days was greatly reduced. It shredded my nerves, reminiscent of the point of collision from the A34. Even now, I still can't tolerate loud noises very well.

I somehow survived the couple of hours of the meal and stood up relieved when it was time to move on. The fresh air allowed me to breathe again, but I could feel my body in a state of fear; it was like being in flight mode at work. It seemed out of context and alien to me – I hadn't put two and two together. Both Daniel and Clara looked at me, concerned, as we stepped out into the streetlights of the town. They talked to me as we walked, worried by the way I was acting. Daniel asked if I wanted to be accompanied back to my car, which was parked at the local fire station about five minutes away, and we both seemed taken aback when I accepted his offer of company. We both knew me to be proudly independent, the person who'd gone on so many solo travels – Daniel had called me a badass in the past for that very reason; that bold streak in my personality. Yet here I was now, shaking, wide-eyed, needing to be escorted a few roads away as I didn't feel safe from myself. We walked and we talked, and he stood with me for a while in the quiet station yard next to my car, until my nerves had calmed and I was once again fit enough to drive. The incident scared me; I felt I was unravelling.

A few days later, it was my next CBT session with Therapist Lady. This was our third virtual meeting, which I found this time to be informative and interesting. We talked about how the brain works and processes memories. My limited understanding from that was that my brain has three main parts to it that were being affected by PTSD. The hippocampus is responsible for organising and stowing memories away; mine had stored memories incorrectly due to the traumatic nature in which they had been created. My brain had been under stress and had kicked into fight-or-flight mode during the crash, so storing the memories was not a priority as it had focused on surviving instead. This had continued into my night shift afterwards. The memories had therefore remained in the wrong place and unprocessed – which meant that my amygdala (the part of the brain responsible for my stress response) now wouldn't get the right signals. It would be extra sensitive when it picked up on certain sounds or sights and would take them as danger cues. It would trigger too easily as the incorrectly stored memories were now being perceived as happening again in real time. This would cause my hypervigilance and would often push me into fight-or-flight mode again.

My prefrontal cortex in the brain is in charge of my emotions. Trauma can make this part underactive and so mine would now struggle to control my emotional responses as it once did. For me this explained why I was feeling all over the place: I'd become quiet at work and short-tempered with my family; sometimes I'd cry, yet sometimes I'd feel completely numb.

Therapist Lady also gave me a worksheet as homework for the week. She wanted me to read through a breakdown of PTSD and its symptoms, annotating if/how each one affected me. I was shocked after reading it – every single symptom seemed to shout at me. They were listed as:

- Re-experiencing – through flashbacks, nightmares

and emotional or bodily reactions

- Physical arousal – fight, flight, freeze
- Dissociation
- Difficulty concentrating
- Fear and anxiety
- Feeling low
- Guilt/shame
- Anger
- Poor self-image and negative thoughts about other people and life
- Isolation
- Pushing memories away
- Dwelling
- Scanning for danger, avoidance and extra precautions
- Using alcohol/other substances
- Numbing emotions

I could identify with all of these. At the time, I didn't seem to experience flashbacks as I understood them to be – although that did change as the months moved on – but I learnt that my being jolted awake by the sound of crashing vehicles was in fact a form of nocturnal flashback. I didn't turn to alcohol or substances; my coping-mechanism equivalent seemed to be work – I was still doing all the overtime I could, even with my symptoms seemingly getting worse. The only step I took to alleviate that situation was to make sure I did extra shifts on Green Watch only, as both Clara and Richard were working there and understood what was going on.

The point on physical arousal was an interesting one; all the notes expanding on this described familiar sensations to me, including being jittery and agitated, overly alert, trembling, having a release of adrenaline, feeling tense, jumpy, irritable and losing my temper easily. Listed were a pounding heart, muscles ready for action, and sleeping trouble – difficulty both dropping off to sleep and remaining asleep throughout the night. I could confirm having every single one of these symptoms. Suddenly it made sense why I'd been referred to seemingly every person in every organisation before the CBT therapy was arranged for me. If I ticked every box, I figured I must be pretty complicated, and this worksheet was proof of that for my own mind.

The next week, I discussed the worksheet as part of the following session with Therapist Lady. She also had some news for me: I would be starting what she called "reliving sessions" in the new year. This provided an answer for me regarding going sick. She explained that these sessions would be difficult; they would be longer – anywhere up to two hours each time – and very intense. She said it would be wise to book sick during this period of therapy, but to aim to go back before our twenty sessions were up to ease my return to the workplace. That sounded like a plan to me, and I was able to give Sam and Keith the heads up too. In the meantime, I prepped with Therapist Lady for reliving, the following week imagining a "safe space" in my mind to retreat to for when I felt things were getting too much within our sessions. My safe space, of course, was the Isle of Wight; a particular clifftop viewpoint overlooking a bay, which was a favourite haunt of mine.

Work seemed to get harder with every shift. My watch were amazingly supportive, as they had been all along. My crew managers, Marcus, Daniel and Lily, and my fellow con-op colleague, Harriet, were particularly kind, offering chats when I needed them, supporting me when I was triggered and sending the odd message of support in an evening after a particularly eventful shift. I was gradually becoming more exhausted as I desperately tried to cling on to being in the workplace, my hopes of being fixed locked on to those promised intense therapy sessions in the new year. I knew I was hard work to be around and I was so glad to have the friends I had. Lunchtime naps seemed to become a thing; I wasn't sleeping well during the night, and riding a wave of adrenaline all morning would leave me shattered by the time my break came around. Even then, I'd still be in hypervigilance mode; a loud noise in the vicinity, for example a door slamming, would jerk me awake in a panic.

Eventually, Christmas came round. I worked an overtime shift on the night of the 23rd, which I didn't realise at the time would be my last extra shift for a while. The hours passed fairly typically, until my commute home the following morning on Christmas Eve. Travelling on the A34 once again – just one junction up from the original trauma crash – I drove past a rollover RTC. My blood ran cold as soon as I spotted it; it wasn't visible until I was almost parallel with it due to the car being upside down on the verge a way up the slope. Because it wasn't easily seen, I had no time or space to stop once I was there. However, I could see that a builder's van had already pulled over and was assisting. This time, my phone was easily accessible; I'd learnt to always keep it in a cradle on the dashboard since witnessing that first A34 crash and not having it to hand. My car also had Bluetooth fitted this time around. I rang into work hands-free and reported the accident. The colleague I spoke to was unaware of my PTSD at this point but I knew Sam and Keith were due to be in the room and would pick up on the fact that it was me reporting an RTC. My brain blocked everything else out; I could hear my voice shaking and I knew my hands were too, but I stayed safe and in the game until I reached the next layby where I could pull the car over. There, I broke down. It took a good forty minutes before I felt stable enough to drive again. The adrenaline surges and the feeling of shock coupled with them made me feel as though I was being struck by lightning bolts continuously.

I waited until my body had stopped trembling and my brain wasn't reeling, shouting at me to flee. Calmer, I drove the remainder of my journey home without incident. Once there, I texted Sam – I couldn't face going to bed without knowing the outcome. I needed to find out how the occupants had fared. Sam replied, giving me the details of the log: it wasn't as serious as my brain had automatically assumed it to be and no one was trapped. She also checked in on me, saying that she and Keith were concerned when they heard it was me calling it in. I assured her I was ok, just shaken, and that I was now home safe.

Christmas day followed. I slept fitfully and when I got up to shower, I realised I felt very wobbly emotionally. This was unusual – I was used to reacting physically, even with tears, but my emotions were often numbed after being triggered. I washed under the hot water while pouring my heart out, feeling wretched and just wanting to go back to bed and curl up in a ball. Still, I forced myself to get ready to walk over to my parents' house, and pasted a smile on my face for the day. It was nice to see the family, though, and Christmas dinner was a triumph as per usual from my dad. On returning home, however, I just felt heavy – kind of sad and empty all at once, and I kept thinking of the rolled-over car and then of the original crash. I cried some more.

I returned to work on Boxing Day. The next couple of tours (set of shifts) seemed to pass in a bit of a shaky blur. I was still being triggered with incidents; I had the newer RTC to process, and my grandad had also been admitted to hospital. This was becoming more of a regular thing as his health grew frailer. He'd been hospitalised for a fall earlier in December and this latest admission, just a few weeks later, led him to catch Covid. It was a concern and my mum's worry for him weighed down on me too. I caught up with Richard at work and offloaded a little, and had further catch-ups with Marcus for the benefit of my watch management, so they'd know what I was struggling with.

I looked forward with anticipation to 7th January 2022: this was the date of my first CBT reliving session. I hoped it would be the start of solving my problems and easing my mindset.

CHAPTER 11
SICKNESS

My appointment with Therapist Lady was scheduled for the afternoon. I was answering standard PHQ-9, GAD-7 and PCL-5 questions every week before my CBT sessions, so she could gauge my progress. This week's results were high, with a trauma score in the fifties, which I felt accurately reflected how I'd been feeling since Christmas Eve. We discussed the events of the previous couple of weeks and then started reliving. This was a form of exposure therapy: she wanted me to pick a starting point, then talk her through the whole evening of the crash in detail but in the present tense, as though it was happening again. I was to describe what I could see, what my actions were and what I was feeling. I'd never gone into details about the crash to anyone before; I was good at glossing over the story without delving in too deep, and I had a habit of discussing it factually, not taking my own perspective into account. Talking it all through with Therapist Lady and filling in the details was extremely hard. I shook and cried; I felt physically triggered the way I would be by RTCs at work.

But Therapist Lady opened up something emotionally too. I was finally starting to connect the dots between what my body was doing and what my brain was shutting down from and refusing to feel. I was a wreck by the end of about ninety minutes. She ensured that our session finished with me feeling calmer, but I was completely wiped out. The massive adrenaline comedown felt again like flu and I was totally drained of energy and of tears.

Once I was finished, I was left reeling. I reached out – texted Daniel and Richard, who both knew I was having my session that day and were waiting to hear about it. I had a long phone conversation with Richard, dissecting everything and discussing the pros and cons of booking sick. Finally, I relented and admitted to myself that I wasn't in a fit state to be working. Instead of my looking at this as a bad thing, he encouraged me to think of it as a break from an environment that could potentially cause me more harm than good. He also told me not to underestimate the effect that intense therapy would have on my mental health.

Richard happened to be on his way to work, so I asked him to book me sick discreetly when he arrived. The normal procedure was to ring in to Control but I couldn't face talking to a different watch about it. I wanted my reasoning to be documented on the sickness form but to remain confidential to my colleagues. Richard did as I asked and also fired off an email to Keith to keep him in the loop following our discussions that evening. I then set about informing those who'd been supporting me.

Everyone was incredibly kind and seemed to agree that this was the best course of action, which was encouraging as I was still wavering over whether it was the right thing to do. I'm rarely ill and never one to book sick, and I knew this was likely to be a prolonged episode of absence. It felt huge and daunting, and it helped knowing so many work friends – particularly those in management roles – believed it was for the best.

I spent the rest of the evening not really knowing what to do with myself. I lit my fire, poured myself a glass of wine and tried to settle myself internally. I was exhausted but wired; very jittery, with shaking hands and my brain going at a hundred miles an hour. I went to bed early but it took a long time to fall asleep.

The following day – a Saturday – was terrible. I spent most of it alternating between a heightened state of nerves and hypervigilance, and crashing out into a fitful sleep. I napped on and off all day. I was incredibly anxious and couldn't concentrate; I couldn't watch television or read any books. I was permanently shaking and just felt exhausted. I was also very wobbly emotionally and I cried a lot. Keeping the curtains closed, I shut the world out and tried to get a control of my body. It was scary. I felt I was breaking down or going crazy – such a massive reaction just from a video chat the day before! And yet, the physical response was somewhat reassuring at the same time: proof to me that I was, in fact, quite ill after all. Debbie had promised to call but I didn't hear from her or receive an apology for her not being able to contact me. I was quite disheartened at this, as she was my watch manager and I hadn't yet had a conversation with her about booking sick.

The next day, Sunday, I had plans to meet up with Georgia and Beth for a walk. I forced myself to go through with it and see my friends, but looking at myself in the mirror before I set off made me doubtful of why I was bothering. My eyes were swollen, bloodshot and dull. This was wrong – my eyes had always been expressive with a bit of a glint to them. I'd never seen them so empty and dark. I was incredibly pale, my skin flaring up with stress. I looked a mess. Nevertheless, I dressed up in warm walking gear and met my friends as intended – then swiftly realised that perhaps this wasn't the best plan. I struggled to look at either of them in the eye, a symptom I was familiar with when triggered at work. I figured I was in a form of flight mode, which would explain why all my senses were screaming at me in hypervigilance.

We walked, and I came clean and explained to them that I'd started therapy and had just booked sick. I broke down completely, sobbing my heart out. They didn't seem to know what to do with this information or with my emotions. To my dismay, they mainly went quiet. Beth asked a few questions and tried to be supportive, but Georgia fell silent and looked scared and unsure. I didn't persist with making them feel uncomfortable and instead the conversation swayed towards safer territory and neutral subjects. However, I came away from that walk a while later feeling devastated. These were some of my oldest friends; I'd confided in them with something personal and raw, and they'd been unable to deal with me.

The day went on and I continued to force myself to "act normal". I was supposed to go to my parents for lunch. I have no idea how I managed to do that without them picking up on how unwell I was. They still had no idea about my diagnosis of PTSD, yet my physical symptoms were glaringly obvious by this point; at least to me. Their dog – a giant Gordon Setter, convinced of being a lapdog – lay across me for most of my visit and hid my trembling hands from sight. I managed a couple of hours in their company before making my excuses and retreating back to the safety of my own home. I felt bad for keeping them in the dark but I couldn't bring myself to say anything. I didn't want to worry them and I couldn't deal with their reaction at that time; I knew it would be well meaning but they'd misunderstand and be overwhelmingly concerned. I'd be ok; I knew I'd be ok. I might be unwell but I had support and I was jumping through the right hoops to improve. Worrying my family wouldn't aid me in that.

I finally received a text from Debbie as I was leaving my parents, and we had our promised chat forty-eight hours later than I'd hoped we would. I know this sounds insignificant but I've always tried to be a person of my word and I felt let down that my manager couldn't offer me the same respect. It was difficult to have to keep repeating myself and I felt I needed to gear up before stressful conversations. I'd quickly learnt I couldn't do this off the cuff. I needed stability, and although I tried to be sympathetic at the time, as I knew Debbie was also going through a turbulent period in her personal life, I struggled with being promised something, psyching myself up for it, and then it not happening.

That second day of sickness ended in more tears: between my civilian friends' horrified reaction, keeping my condition secret from my parents, and my short, belated conversation with Debbie, I felt pretty isolated by the time evening fell.

My week continued in much the same way. It felt as though I was falling apart at the seams. I tried going into the supermarket and nearly cried in the milk aisle. My senses were in overdrive; I hated the noise, the bustle, the people. I flinched and jumped at everything around me and was overwhelmed by my whole environment. For a good few days, I shook continuously, then intermittently for the rest of the week.

When I spoke to Sasha and Lucy, they were amazing. Sasha was working from home and, despite having video conferences booked for the day, she invited me round for a cuppa on the Tuesday. I kept out of sight of her computer's camera and let her work, but between meetings we caught up, we talked and we drank copious amounts of tea. I felt a bit as though I was in shock; I was honest with her but not overly forthcoming with conversation. I was safe to feel vulnerable and be in company with someone who was happy to listen and support; equally, I could just sit there and not say anything.

Sasha sent me home with food parcels of homemade curry, which was very kind. I wasn't really eating a lot. The stress and anxiety took my appetite away and left me feeling nauseous. Lucy then visited me the following afternoon. Being Sasha's daughter, they had obviously had a discussion about my situation, as she came laden with further meals; easy convenience food that I could ping in the microwave with no effort. I was overwhelmed by their thoughtfulness and it was lovely to see her.

And so, the days ticked on. I had another reliving CBT session about ten days later, which felt as brutal as the first. The physical come down from that seemed slightly easier this time round, or at least, the shaking stopped more quickly. I researched and found trauma/PTSD groups online and on social media – people I could read about and learn from, which helped me realise that everything I was feeling and experiencing was part of the condition and was normal. There were stories of therapy successes, which offered hope for improvement; some brutally honest venting, which I could often identify with; and some posts full of dark humour, something I could very much get on board with. Lucy and I started swapping the most shocking of these to keep my spirits up.

I had no energy for anything really and just felt shattered – it seemed the months I'd spent feeling tense at work were finally catching up with me now I'd stopped to rest. Despite this, I tasked myself over the next week with stripping my small bathroom of its manky wallpaper. I had contractors already booked in to redo the room for me, arranged when I moved into the house. Frustratingly, however, this now coincided with my being off sick and generally wanting to avoid people. Nevertheless, the building work was going ahead so I had to prep the room. I tried to do a little every day. I also knew that fresh air was good for me but couldn't face going out walking or exercising.

Instead, I spent a lot of mornings in the cold January air, sitting on my back doorstep, with a tea in hand, letting the rabbits roam the garden and watching their antics. This, I felt, would get the approval of the Fire Fighters Charity for ticking the mindfulness box!

Stress had completely taken over my body. I looked dead behind the eyes. My skin had flared worse than ever, my hair was falling out, and I was now having allergic reactions. Our family have always had allergies; seemingly random swellings of various body parts with no obvious cause. I was learning that, for me, stress was a triggering factor – only now, not only did I have to contend with my hands or feet or face swelling up, I also had angry hives that appeared over my body. Antihistamines seemed to reduce the reactions, but it felt as though I was having to eat them like sweets to keep my body on an even keel. My watch had been back at work and, again, I was promised a phone call from Debbie, which never happened. This time it was due to her being needed to help with trainees in the workplace. I understood that she was busy – but I didn't understand why she didn't tell me that, or delegate welfare duties to a crew manager if she didn't have capacity, instead of just not making contact.

I had plans to meet up with Lucy again a few days after talking to Therapist Lady for the second time, so I was quite surprised when Sasha rang me the night before. Lucy had suffered a medical trauma, had lost quite a lot of blood and was rather unwell. This news winded me and filled me with dread. I messaged her straight away; we talked for a bit and I offered to visit her when she was well enough. A few days after the event, I drove to see her. This time, it was me bringing food and some flowers too. I felt guilty that I'd been sending her black-humoured texts when, unbeknownst to me, she'd been in hospital. However, it turned out she'd been glad to receive them. So we continued, with Lucy relating to them just as much as I did now.

We fell into a good routine, supporting each other: Lucy's illness was physically debilitating for a long while, which meant she was unable to drive. I, however, insisted to myself that I must continue to use my car. I knew that if I stopped, I'd quite likely develop a phobia of driving and would struggle to start again. I needed to stay brave enough to remain a safe and competent driver. I also knew that arranging to visit Lucy, who needed support, would help me too. It was very easy to hide at home and not see anyone, but knowing she couldn't come to me pushed me into remaining a little sociable. We lived nearly an hour apart, so the journey each way was a challenge. But I'm an incredibly stubborn person and understood that, despite my hypervigilance, driving that distance was doing me good. My heightened awareness, I believed, led me to be a safer driver too.

And so it went on: we'd get together every week and I'd take advantage of the opportunity to pop round to see Sasha too. Both these women were an immeasurable support in my PTSD recovery and I owe them so much.

Bathroom demolition began on 24th January. I'd had no idea how much this would affect me. First, the noise: I was unable to tolerate loud bangs; my body would jump and it almost felt as though my whole brain flinched. It seemed to me I was hearing the crash again, over and over. Breaking up an entire bathroom suite and fitting a new one is noisy work. When the builders left after their first day, I was already at my wits' end. Secondly, my allergies went into overdrive and I was a shaky, nervous wreck. But I had to try to hold it together – although I was in my own home, I wasn't in a safe space to be crying or having a breakdown while there were tradespeople there.

The work ended up taking longer than anticipated – probably two and a half weeks overall. For half that time, I had no working toilet plumbed in. This, on the face of it, wasn't as bad as it sounded – my parents lived round the corner and I was able to use their facilities whenever I needed to. However, this also meant that I had to put a brave face on several times a day. I was shaky, distressed, my nerves absolutely frayed, yet I had to appear "normal" whenever I popped in. I had to explain, too, why I wasn't at work every day – my excuse was that I was taking annual leave to supervise the building work. I hated lying; I especially hated this pit of lies I seemed to be digging myself into with my family – but in my eyes, it was still better than having to talk through everything with them.

I escaped the house two days later and visited Daniel and Clara, following their kind offer to meet me for a cuppa. They both lived in the same town, at the other end of the county from where I was. As they were both on-call firefighters, it made sense for me to travel to them while they maintained cover.

Daniel invited me to meet him to take his dog for a walk before heading to the coffee shop, an offer I gratefully accepted. We walked across empty fields with Isla the Labrador, who was still a young dog and a welcome distraction from my racing thoughts. We talked frankly; I seemed to be able to open up to some people more than others, and friends like Daniel, Clara and, indeed, Richard all had operational firefighting experience, so seemed to "get it" more than others. Daniel hadn't suffered from PTSD himself, but he had friends who had, and seemed to empathise where others perhaps couldn't. We spoke about his own health too – he was awaiting an operation, due in a couple of weeks, and was part way through a long journey of his own. It was an emotional hour and I was able to cry and shake, while walking in the cold air worked its magic. I hoped that Daniel benefitted too by being able to voice his own troubles. He was shortly due to be booking sick himself because of his upcoming surgery, and the two of us being "sick buddies" at the same time seemed to help immeasurably.

Daniel offered to put me in touch with a friend of his, Jon, who had first-hand experience of what I was going through. I was sceptical as, up until now, my struggles had remained a tight secret within only a select few. But I promised to consider it and Daniel later sent me a video link of Jon giving a public talk about his own experiences with PTSD.

We eventually finished the walk and met up with Clara. It was lovely to see her and I was grateful that at my lowest ebb – and I knew I was a mess at this point! – my friends were there for me.

My next CBT session was scheduled for when the bathroom was still in progress on 30th January. Lucy kindly invited me to conduct the video session at her house instead, away from the banging and the contractors overhearing. This is what I did, then I retreated to Sasha's house to find them both once I'd finished. It was a surreal moment: Lucy and I sat together at the dining table, both seemingly in a state of shock for different reasons, with Sasha doing her best to support us.

I felt numb. I was a few sessions into reliving by now, yet every one of them seemed to hit just as hard; seemed just as difficult to talk through. When exactly could I expect to make some progress? I'd hit my highest trauma score yet, this time round scoring sixty-two points out of eighty. I felt the most vulnerable I'd ever been. The only improvement I seemed to note was that the persistent shaking straight after a CBT session appeared to ease a little sooner with each week. I still felt incredibly low, anxious and tearful. I still couldn't eat or sleep properly; or focus on much for a period of time; or withstand the world around me without hypervigilance overwhelming me. I was still having intrusive thoughts, nightmares and nocturnal flashbacks. Even watching things on television became risky – if a crash happened on the telly that I wasn't expecting, it would send me into a spin and I'd be triggered. I couldn't tolerate music I wasn't braced for; a banging beat would send my senses into overdrive. This meant I stuck to the familiar: I'd watch the same "safe" TV shows over and over; listen to my own playlist in the car repeatedly, and not the radio. If I knew what was coming, it lessened a reaction from me. But this scared and frustrated me, as someone who had always been so outgoing and confident – now I wasn't even brave enough to listen to the radio? I'd had enough of reliving those poor people's deaths over and over in my head. I'd had enough of being scared to sleep and unable to drop off; of staying up until I physically couldn't keep my eyes open any longer to stave off the inevitable terror as soon as I got into bed. When would this end?

CHAPTER 12
COPING

I rang my doctor the next day to extend my sickness. I could hardly believe I'd been off for nearly a month already. She was very good in our telephone appointment, listening to everything and reassuring me that things were progressing as they should. I was still unmedicated and she was of the opinion that that was the best course of action for me while I was still in therapy. From my understanding, medications could help me manage the symptoms – but the whole point of exposure therapy and reliving sessions was to open myself up to my symptoms, and to process and learn to manage my condition. Masking what I was feeling was only going to be detrimental to my progress in CBT.

The doctor extended my sickness for a further four weeks, with a plan to check in after that. I also received a message from Keith, which was very kind.

He asked how I was doing and I was able to pass on my sick note to him. I believe he felt a sense of responsibility as he was the one who'd recognised my PTSD symptoms and started the whole ball rolling. I felt nothing but gratitude, though, that he'd noticed what was wrong and supported me in getting help. He promised to check in again soon. Sam had messaged and called several times, too, which was very considerate. I hadn't expected either of them to touch base with me, being control managers, let alone more frequently than my own watch manager did. I was humbled that they'd thought of me.

I met up with Amy a couple of days later, once my physical symptoms had again calmed down following my latest session. It was lovely to see her and catch up properly, although the role reversal seemed strange after my visits to her when she was sick the previous year! By now, she'd been given a diagnosis and was slowly regaining strength and adapting to her new disability. It was great that she was now well enough to drive and meet up for lunch. I offloaded a lot on her and tried to keep my hypervigilance at bay while we were in a restaurant, which fortunately was pretty empty.

The following day, I'd made plans to catch up with Lily and Harriet from work, and Debbie was coming along too. It was good to see them all, although rather daunting to be meeting several people at once. We met in a town that was mutually distant from all of us and only fifteen minutes away from Daniel's house, so my plan was to visit him too before heading home. Lunch with the three of them was overwhelming but much appreciated. It was great to talk in person about how things were going, though I struggled to remain calm in the busy pub where we'd chosen to eat. I had to take antihistamines as my allergies took over yet again due to the stress. I wasn't overly chatty, trying to normalise my breathing and calm my heart palpitations, and my shaking hands were very obvious. Still, it was good to be surrounded by them all; I'd missed my work colleagues since being off sick.

They took it all in their stride and promised to arrange another lunch date soon. I then carried on the few minutes to Daniel's house, and enjoyed puppy cuddles from Isla. Daniel's son was poorly and off nursery, so I had a little friend showing me his games on his tablet. It was a wonderful distraction and chatting to Daniel was a tonic as always. He was only a few days away from finishing work himself, his operation looming. We again discussed my meeting up with his friend, Jon; I'd been thinking about it a lot.

By the time I got home that evening, I was exhausted. Riding my adrenaline spikes throughout lunch, then a frank, emotional talk with Daniel had left me shattered. After a sleep and some thinking, though, I messaged him to agree that, yes, I would meet his friend – on the condition that Daniel accompany me for some moral support. It would likely be organised for after his surgery date, so I left it with the boys to arrange.

My sickness continued into February. I wasn't sure how my parents hadn't realised by now that I wasn't going to work; I only lived in the next road on, which my dad passed most days to take the dog for a walk. My car was bright purple and incredibly recognisable. Somehow though, between taking "leave" or "swapping my shift", if they ever asked, I was still getting away with few questions. I was grateful for this but continued to feel guilty – even though my grandad was now extremely poorly so my mum was already stressed to her maximum without knowing of my issues. I didn't have the heart to put those on her too.

My CBT continued weekly-ish; I still struggled to see how I was progressing, and found the reliving sessions just as hard. I continued to visit Lucy and Sasha, while weekly dog walks with Daniel and Isla had become a thing. We met one last time before his surgery was due in mid-February. He was likely to be in hospital for about a week and would have reduced mobility for a while after that. I worried for him – it seemed my stress overflowed into other life events too. I struggled to keep my panic at bay whenever Lucy was having a very sick day; now my nerves were strung out for a second friend. Nevertheless, I messaged him the day before he was admitted onto the ward, then refrained from sending him anything more until he was ready to reach out and converse. I refused to let my panic take over. I knew he had his family supporting him and was in safe hands; that I would be told if there were any complications. Thankfully, it all went fine and he recovered remarkably well.

I tried to keep myself busy and distracted from my jitters, putting some more effort into my doer-upper house – this time trying to remove the stuck-on laminate from the hallway floor that covered beautiful original tiles. My parents also asked me to assist in decorating their spare bedroom on my "days off" – I find painting very relaxing, and this distracted further. I could plug my music in, shut the door and absorb myself in the task at hand.

I met up with an old friend I've known since school. Our social get-togethers were often a little sporadic but it was wonderful to see her all the same. I caught up with another colleague as well, Alison, who had been my watch manager when I was on White Watch for a couple of years. She didn't know the reasons behind my absence from work, but had noted I'd been off sick for a few weeks, so very kindly reached out offering to meet for coffee. We met in a garden centre café situated between the two of us. She seemed shocked to see me trembling bodily and initially thought I was shaking with cold. I told her the whole story of my PTSD. It was difficult running through it again with someone new, but I felt she deserved the truth considering she was willing to meet me without knowing what had happened. We spent a good couple of hours chatting and I came away feeling drained, but glad to have another friend by my side.

That evening, Lily messaged to check in. I chose to pick her brains about something Daniel had mentioned. He'd been allocated a welfare officer now he was off sick, arranged through his on-call employment, but they were also keeping Control up to date. I wondered if I was meant to have an official welfare officer. I'd talked a lot with several friends from work via messages and phone calls but that was on a social basis as opposed to a formal one.

Earlier that day, I'd received two notifications from Occupational Health. This was the service responsible for assisting with an employee's health and wellbeing. They informed me they had arranged and then rearranged appointments for me at the request of my employer – but who had asked for these to be scheduled and then moved? I certainly hadn't had that conversation. I assumed it was going through Debbie. However, we were mid-February now and, apart from at the lunch she'd joined with Lily and Harriet, I'd only spoken twice with Debbie (on the phone) in the one and a half months I'd been off sick. There had been no messaging or chit-chat in between. Lily was working a night shift that evening with Debbie, so said she would ask her about it. Debbie responded to me via text the following morning. She informed me that the appointment had been moved as HR wanted it to be sooner. She said she was due to go on leave for the next couple of weeks but to contact her or Lily if I had any issues. I was also to think about what I was going to do with my sickness at the end of the month.

Suddenly, I felt like a bit of an inconvenience to her, although I didn't really understand why I would be. I'd tried not to be needy or high maintenance; I hadn't reached out or bothered her at all. I knew she was under a lot of pressure from her own workload; that Control had been crazy busy recently and she also had her own stresses outside the work environment. But ultimately, she was my boss and I was her responsibility. It had taken a lot for me to finally agree to book sick. There was no way I was going to be rushed back into work before I was ready. I realised I was probably reading more into Debbie's text than was there, particularly with my emotions all over the place. But I did feel it was rather a harsh thing to write and I definitely took it to heart more than I would have normally have done.

Storm Eunice hit the UK that Friday. I felt guilty

and useless, sitting at home watching it out of my window when I should have been at work, helping. I knew the mobilising system was having some issues and that crewing levels were low. I knew, too, that morale wasn't good and my friends would all be stretched and struggling to deal with the catastrophic effects of such a big storm. But it was all out of my control.

I "rescued" half a tree that broke off outside my house, and used a small handsaw to cut the branches up for firewood and rabbit chews. The pictures of my chopped-up tree stacked neatly in piles seemed to amuse my friends a little at least, and doing the work kept me distracted from my thoughts.

The next week was a tricky one for me. It started off all right, with Amy feeling well enough to come and see my new house for the first time. It was my birthday the following day so, traditionally, Georgia, Beth and I would meet up around that time as we all had birthdays within a few weeks of each other. This year, it felt a bit rocky, though – after pouring my heart out to them the same weekend I booked sick, I hadn't heard from either of them in over a month. I messaged them when they finally starting talking about getting together, explaining that, while I didn't want an argument or to blame anyone, their silence had really upset me when they were supposed to be close friends. They apologised, and I had a very frank discussion with Beth, who revealed she was struggling with her own mental wellbeing. Our chat prompted her to do something about it. She ended up being referred for help via her GP, so our talk did some good.

Georgia was apologetic but had no reason for

vanishing off the radar other than being busy. I suspected my whole situation was majorly out of her comfort zone, though that didn't excuse her in my eyes. Living with PTSD wasn't exactly fun for me either – surely friends were supposed to support each other when times became tough?

The three of us met at Beth's house the evening before my thirty-first birthday. I knew I was withdrawn and separate from the conversation happening around me. I felt numb; kind of detached from the two of them, yet strangely close to tears the whole evening. When I got home afterwards, I cried. What should have been an enjoyable birthday celebration with friends was very, very difficult.

I gave Georgia a lift there and back. She was clearly nervous and wouldn't address the elephant in the room, instead talking a lot about her car and other inconsequential things to fill the silence. She didn't once ask me how I was doing. Beth tried her best to keep the conversation going through the evening. She messaged me the following day too and we chatted. But I felt as though my illness was changing the course of my friendship with them both; I could feel the distance growing between the three of us.

The week continued: my birthday the next day was spent with my family in the morning, which was nice, and I had afternoon plans to see Lucy and pop in to see Sasha too. What I didn't realise was that, between the two of them, they'd planned a birthday tea for me, including a homemade birthday cake from Lucy. I was so touched – she wasn't doing a lot of cooking as she was still very poorly and generally couldn't stand in the kitchen for long. So for her to push through and make me a cake from scratch must have taken an enormous amount of effort and pain. She and Sasha were both amazing and, just as they had for my thirtieth, they made my birthday special despite the circumstances surrounding it.

The week spiralled as it continued. I had another reliving session, which was hard and left me wobbly. I then had a phone conversation with Sam, but what was meant to be a nice catch-up ended up triggering me quite badly. We somehow got on to the subject of my booking sick. There was a box to tick to determine if it was a work-related sickness or not. I'd asked Richard to tick this box when he filled in the form and he'd done so. This had apparently been overruled and changed by work – I believe discussions were had between my managers and HR – as they determined that, because I had witnessed the A34 crash on the way into work and my shift hadn't yet commenced, this wasn't a work-related illness. In real terms it changed nothing for me: I was still entitled to full pay when off sick and I would still be supported. To me personally, though, it made a massive difference. It felt as though the brigade was dismissing my PTSD. They didn't seem to understand that, yes, the original collision took place before my shift, but I then continued to work that shift for a full fifteen hours afterwards and had to deal with that same incident. I believed – as did Therapist Lady – that it was the combination of both which was the cause of the condition and it was frustrating that work wouldn't recognise that. I ended up having a long phone conversation with Richard a few hours afterwards. I was upset and needed to vent after an emotional week.

The next day, I had my first Occupational Health appointment. I found this to be upsetting, too, on an already fragile mindset, as I talked through my current symptoms and what I perceived to be limited progress so far. No recommendations were offered at this point, as I was intending to remain off sick for the time being. I was asked to get back in touch nearer to the time I'd be looking to return to work.

I spent the weekend in quite a fraught state, the conversations (or lack of them!) with Georgia and Beth, Occupational Health and Sam all circling my mind, on the back of a heavy therapy session. I tried to calm myself but I was tense and jittery, full of anxiety and heart palpitations that seemed to work my brain into a frenzy. I let off some steam talking with Daniel on the Monday following. It was good to catch up with both him and his wife as he recuperated at home.

The next day, Blue Watch were on shift and Lily, in Debbie's absence, had decided to welfare-call me. It was a relief to have a formal, scheduled check-in from work for once, but I'd worked myself into such a state over the events of the last few days that I ended up just crying down the phone at her. She seemed very concerned, reporting my teary state to Keith, who promised to call me the following day.

Lily was worried I was becoming depressed. She texted me later and the next day too, urging me to have a check-in with my GP. Other watch members also messaged me, so I realised I must have worried her quite a bit. I tried to reassure her once I'd calmed down a little and my chat with Keith had settled me further. I explained that I'd had a tense week of being overwhelmed and repeatedly triggered. I knew I wasn't depressed; my moods were just very up and down, and correlated directly to events around me in an exaggerated fashion. I explained to her that PTSD involved mood swings and dips in emotion. Unfortunately, she'd caught me in the midst of a real low after a period of time with little sleep and my brain fretfully tying itself in knots.

CHAPTER 13
IMPROVING

So, time moved on. February turned into March, and my emotions started to stabilise. Nightmares reduced in frequency, although sleep still wasn't good. I repeatedly tried to push myself out of my comfort zone, and insisted on driving to visit friends to continue to face my demons. My stubborn self wouldn't let my PTSD completely overwhelm my mind. It would have been very easy to hole myself up at home and never leave the house, and never drive my car. I refused to allow either of those things to happen.

Both Daniel and Lucy seemed to improve as the weeks passed, and I carried on my regular visits to them. I met Clara and Lily again too – I was still very shaky in public, but felt more forthcoming when it came to talking about my situation. Lily had adopted an unofficial welfare role for me in work and continued to call me each week. I found that reliability reassuring.

With a further sick note, I also decided it was finally time to tell my parents. I hated continually lying to them and wasn't sure if they'd picked up by now that things weren't ringing true. I timed it well – just before the dog was due his walk – so I knew he'd be pestering to leave and my chat would be brief. They both reacted exactly as I expected them to. I told them I was booked sick and that it was due to PTSD from work, but I didn't go into details. My mum looked grief-stricken. I tried to sound light-hearted, making a joke about even having my own therapist, but at that knowledge, she seemed to visibly panic. Having therapy and going to my GP, apparently, was very serious and not good.

My dad's response was a well-meaning but practical one, first to check I was still receiving wages – which, thankfully, I was – and then to ask why I didn't just find a new job if my current one was stressing me out. I tried to stay calm as I answered that but his comment frustrated me nonetheless. I liked my job. I thought I was quite good at my job. If I chose to leave, then it would be my decision made with a stable mind, and not a knee-jerk reaction because I was unwell; my illness forcing me out was a very last resort to me. Besides, I knew that just leaving wouldn't fix the damage already done: I had PTSD now and it wasn't going away anytime soon. I knew, too, that my current workplace would support me through this more than any other kind of employer would be able to. My dad's comments came from a good place and he meant well but he didn't understand.

The following couple of weeks were tricky. My dad

took it upon himself to ring and text me multiple times every day, "just for a chat". The phone calls were about inconsequential things and were his way of checking I was ok. He was clearly worried. Only, I didn't want to be badgered all day, every day. I was managing and didn't need frequent calls or mollycoddling. I tried to be patient and reasoned to myself that I'd had many months to wrap my head around this, whereas my family were just learning about it. It was sweet that he was so concerned and I didn't want to be ungrateful; I held my tongue for that reason. But I really wanted the sudden influx of calls to stop. I'd go to my parents if I needed them; being pestered wasn't helping me.

The calls abated somewhat two weeks later: my elderly grandad passed away. He'd been poorly for a long time all through the pandemic, so it wasn't a surprise and was very peaceful. Nevertheless, it floored my mum, who now had to deal with the funeral, his house sale and most of his affairs, on top of her own grief. This, naturally, distracted my dad as he now needed to be there for her.

The funeral was scheduled for the end of the month. I tried to be supportive but found I had a limited capacity. I took my mum clothes shopping for the service and helped her clear out some of the house; I could focus on practical tasks. Emotional support, however, was something I struggled with. I seemed to have reached my quota; I had nothing left to give. Looking back, I can see I should have been there more; I tried to check in frequently but I know I held myself at a bit of a distance and put barriers up. It was hard enough dealing with my own trauma, deaths that still weighed so heavily on me every day. I was already trying to handle two poorly friends, albeit that the care was reciprocated and they had their respective families looking after them too. It still took up space and worry in my brain. I couldn't deal very well with extra loss on top of everything else. This is a regret I have to this day – I know I should have been there for my mum more.

Meanwhile, as my symptoms started to improve, Therapist Lady came up with a plan: my sickness was extended into the beginning of April but after that, I would try a phased return back into the workplace while I still had a number of therapy sessions left to support the transition. We both realised that progress would stagnate without my eventually putting myself back in the environment that triggered me so much, therefore being able to test where I was in my recovery and addressing my reactions as they happened. She recommended I try to visit Control a couple of times for a cuppa, to reacclimatise myself gradually and see if I was near the point of being ready to return. I had a date in the diary to finally have that promised talk with Jon. He worked at a fire station about fifteen minutes from Daniel's house. My plan was to meet them both, then head on to Control that afternoon, since I would already have driven part of the route already.

I arrived early on the day to calm my nerves and recover from my drive. Daniel and I took Isla for a quick walk in the fresh air, before he drove me to the station after a slight change of plan. The watch were there having their tea break when we arrived – not a problem, and I felt quite at home in a fire station setting; but I was aware I probably looked a bit of a state and I was rather self-conscious trying not to alarm them with my shaking, or general demeanour, which was still visibly hypervigilant.

I recognised a lot of myself in Jon's words. His PTSD was also work related. How he felt, his journey through it and his symptoms all mirrored my experience. It was a relief to talk to someone about it without having to explain myself – he just got it. He asked questions: about my habits and how I was coping; about my therapy; about my support from family and friends; about how it affected work and how I intended to return. It also helped massively that he was familiar with the A34 crash that had initiated all this – his particular station housed one of the crews that attended the scene, although it was a different watch and he personally didn't deal with it. He told me that the crews even now didn't talk about that crash; never had. That settled in my head a little that the magnitude of the collision wasn't just my take on it; it wasn't simply a weakness of my own mind. It clearly was a devastating event that had a wide-rippling effect on everyone involved; even those attending in a professional capacity avoided thinking about it, as I had done for so many years.

Our chat, unfortunately, was cut short; the bells went down as the watch got called out to a shout. It was the first time I'd heard a station turnout since my PTSD diagnosis, and my whole body immediately freaked. It was an instant surge of adrenaline: I shook; every muscle was trembling. I was tensed and sweating, breathing fast, my heart racing. Even more alarming, though, was that my head seemed to have caught up with my body being triggered: weeks of trauma therapy had brought my emotions and my thinking to the surface. Up until booking sick, my feelings had been buried and resulted in my having a purely physical reaction to triggers. Now I was having flashbacks; my whole being filled with horror, and panic, and dread. My hands instinctively reached to hold my head and I felt frantic, torn; wanting to move and run away and instead being rooted to my seat, not being able to move at all; desperately trying to clutch and hide my head from the terror it was experiencing.

The crew jumped up to leave. Jon took one look at me and fired an instruction to Daniel to look after me, before he, too, had to respond to the fire call. Daniel was amazing, staying by my side while I tried to ride out everything that had taken me over. My surroundings seemed to fade into insignificance and I was totally zoned into what was going on internally. It almost felt as if there was a blockage at the front of my brain; something physical that stopped me from talking. I couldn't think or move consciously and my body took over on autopilot.

After a while – it seemed like a lifetime but was probably twenty to thirty minutes – I was calmer; drained to exhaustion but back in control. We stayed and had a further cup of tea until I'd regained stability, and discussed the options for the afternoon. I was still insistent on visiting Control – I'd tried to arrange it for the week before but my plans hadn't come to fruition due to last-minute crewing levels, so I was reluctant to cancel again. I knew I was running out of time before I had to make a decision about whether I was ready to book fit and return to work. My visit was important to gauge where I was in my recovery and to test my reaction in the control room. Daniel very kindly drove me and accompanied me while I was there.

Control was hard. I'd given my watch the heads-up on when we were visiting and I messaged them en route too – I knew there were trainees working that day and I wasn't keen on them being in the room if I ended up having a meltdown on my first visit back. The training manager was understanding about this and made sure they weren't working in the control room on my arrival.

When Daniel pulled up into the car park, my blood ran cold. I was anxious and shaky, and I seemed to withdraw into myself. Nevertheless, I forced myself through the doors and into the control room. My watch were pleased to see me; Clara was there too, doing overtime. The day was a quiet one with no RTCs in progress while I was there, so I got the space to readjust. Our visit lasted about an hour and a half. I flinched and froze whenever the phone rang and my heart jumped with a jolt of adrenaline, but overall I managed ok.

I also had a chat with Sam in her office. I went to find her as she was finishing talking with Daniel, so we ended up having a meeting all together. Sam was very keen to get me back in the workplace as soon as I felt able, but I got the impression she still didn't realise the full implications of my illness. I explained to her that I would struggle returning at a time when the crewing was so poor – even as a supernumerary member of staff. That was a lot of pressure to jump straight back into. I needed more time to adjust to just being in the room and dealing with my own reaction to the jobs around me, without the staffing levels pressurising me into moving too fast. Sam offered to switch me to a watch that had a better crewing level – Blue Watch were currently being hit hard by a bout of sickness – but I instantly dismissed that. It was Blue Watch who had been supporting me all along; they knew how this was progressing. I couldn't drop that rapport and start again with a whole new group of colleagues. She also tried to suggest that maybe I was only reacting due to the anticipation of a call, and getting myself worked up – Daniel shot down that train of thought by describing how that morning at the fire station had played out for me.

Sam then proposed that I could work outside the control room for a period of time, completing paperwork if it got too much. Again, I tried to explain that that wouldn't work. I needed to expose myself to my triggers in order to overcome them. I also couldn't focus on anything, even mundane paperwork, if I was overwhelmed.

Finally, she had the idea of joining me on one of my therapy sessions to speak to Therapist Lady about my return to work. This was a definite no from me – my sessions were confidential and very raw; I didn't want anyone intruding on them. I knew I needed to be in my own workspace with my own watch for this to work, but with less pressure on me to actually do the job until I was more resilient. I was to speak to Keith the following day about this.

I came away from Control shortly afterwards feeling totally drained, proud, terrified and frustrated. I was glad to have faced my fears and to have visited, and it was wonderful to see my colleagues again after nearly three months. But I felt wound up that Sam couldn't quite understand what I was trying to explain – and yet touched that she was attempting to find solutions to help me regardless. She meant well and was doing her best to support me, despite not fully grasping the gravity of the situation. I also felt cross and frustrated with myself – I wanted to be better and calmer than I was. I was incredibly anxious just from sitting and doing nothing. There was a lot of pressure and doubt coming from my own mind now over whether I could beat this and return to my job and my life fully, or whether things would have to drastically change if I simply couldn't cope. That thought terrified me. But I knew my reaction that morning had been a huge one and I couldn't ignore that.

Being triggered at the fire station and then being on tenterhooks all afternoon had left me exhausted. I was grateful to Daniel for driving me while I pulled myself together, and I napped as soon as I returned home.

The following day, I spoke to Keith on the phone. The visit to Control had made me realise I needed a lot more exposure in the room before I would be capable of taking calls. I recounted to him my experience with the fire station turnout, and my afternoon afterwards. He agreed that we needed to tread slowly with my return to work and was happy for the first couple of tours to consist of my just coping with being in the room – no headset on but simply adjusting to the environment around me. There was absolutely no pressure from Keith and I was grateful he was aware that my phased return was likely to be protracted.

A few days later, I headed back to the fire station with Daniel to finish talking with Jon. This time, we excused ourselves from the rest of the watch and found a quiet room upstairs. We talked for about two hours. I was keen to learn how he managed himself day-to-day: how did he cope with the constant hypervigilance? How did he remain in control and level-headed when triggered? We discussed things at great length – coping strategies, therapies, ways of thinking. I explained my experience of my visit to Control. I also revealed how terrified I was to just travel to work: soon I would be back commuting past the site of the crash twice a day; a route I hadn't done since booking sick. I was scared my therapy would have affected my capacity to deal with that stretch of road, and I shed a few tears while talking. Jon came up with the suggestion of my driving there with Daniel, taking the opportunity to be accompanied by someone. That particular junction had a layby further up, and a slip road with a farm track off it at the bottom of the hill; both places would allow a car to pull over safely. Once I'd done the journey and stopped and absorbed the road with a friend, it might make my route easier to travel in future. Just the thought of it seemed to turn my blood to ice. And yet, the plan made sense. It was better to face this now, with someone, and stop and deal with it, than drive it on my own in a couple of weeks and not know how I would cope.

So, I agreed.

Jon had to stay at station due to being on duty. Daniel and I bid him goodbye and headed off in Daniel's car. We decided it would be a safer option for him to drive, as my reaction was unknown. Daniel drove to the A34, the site of the crash being only a couple of junctions on from where we were. As soon as we crested the top of the hill, I could feel my mind shutting my emotions down. It was remaining in survival mode: normally if I was in the car and driving, it was necessary to push feelings and reactions away to concentrate and remain safe. I could feel tears welling up; I felt very jittery; but I was still in control.

We drove down the hill, off the slip road and parked up a short distance away. Then we walked back the way we'd come, up the wide, grassy verge that led up the slip road and on to the corner where it meets the junction. We stopped, and my eyes locked on to the carriageway ahead. We were at the bottom of the hill on the southbound side but we had a perfect view of the whole stretch. I was fixated on the spot in the opposite direction, about a third of the way from the top of the hill, where I knew the collision had happened.

In that instant, I broke. I could see the lorry climbing the hill, way too fast; I could hear the loud bang reverberating through my head; and I could see the vehicles all colliding, one into the other. I was there; it was happening again in front of me. Horror, fear, panic, dread all coursed through my veins; emotional flashbacks seemed stronger than anything visual. I couldn't speak; I couldn't move; I stood tensed, bracing myself for the impact, absorbing the collision, shaking uncontrollably. Tears poured out.

Daniel once again picked up the broken pieces of me. I stood there, everything washing over me; not really aware of anything much in the present other than the vehicles which thundered past, every whoosh of a car causing me to flinch. But I could feel the weight of Daniel's arm across my shoulders, which gradually pulled me back into the now. We didn't speak; I couldn't, he didn't have to. He let me take as long as I needed and we stayed there as I withstood the onslaught of my senses.

After some time, my mind was able to function again and I was ready to leave. I was very wobbly walking the short distance back to the car, my whole body exhausted from bracing and from bearing the flood of adrenaline through my veins. Once we got to the vehicle, it felt as though I shut down totally. I was numb, wiped out, and the journey back to Daniel's house seemed to happen without my really registering it. We spoke briefly about what I'd just experienced, then I lapsed into silence, unable to properly follow a conversation. I felt almost detached from everything around me; I would describe it as a kind of dissociation. Back at Daniel's house, his wife made me a cup of tea. I sat on their living room floor, hugging Isla the dog, still feeling very off and extremely drained. It took a while before I felt human enough to drive back home safely.

The following day, it was the funeral for my grandad. I knew this was going to be tricky for me; my emotions weren't really stable enough to withstand what was ahead. Regardless, there was no option but to go through it. I'd already told my parents I wasn't going to the gathering at the local pub afterwards; that I would take my own car and drive myself home once we'd finished at the crematorium. I knew my mum was gutted about this but it was for her benefit as much as for my own – I didn't know how well I'd be able to navigate the day and didn't want to make it harder for her. This day was for my grandad and for his children;

not for me, and certainly not for my PTSD to take the limelight.

I arrived at the crematorium in good time and reacquainted with extended family I hadn't seen in a long while. I repeated again to my parents when asked that I wouldn't be joining them after the service, trying not to sound too harsh in doing so. The funeral itself reflected the loving man my grandad was. I sat next to my sister and found myself comforting her, pulling her head into my body as she cried. Tears silently poured down my own face.

After saying goodbye for the final time, and appreciating all the beautiful notes and flowers that had been left in tribute, I found my dad, who once again asked if I couldn't change my mind about joining everyone for a drink. I looked over to my mum. She was with my uncle and still crying, and I realised I couldn't really say no. I felt so terribly guilty. No answer was the right answer: if I refused, then I would be the horrible person who'd bailed early on my grandad's funeral. If I said yes, then I knew my PTSD would take over on what should have been a day of supporting my mum and her brothers.

I finally relented and agreed that I would show for half an hour. I drove there, absolutely torn and just wanting to return home to the silent safety of my house. Instead, I sat with my family as they talked about my grandad and my nan, and caught up on their own family lives. I remained there, silent, unable to join in conversations; hypervigilant to the hubbub going on around me in the slightly echoey pub and trying to remain grounded enough not to let my emotions take over. I couldn't eat as my stomach was tied in knots, which I could see upset my dad as he had arranged the buffet spread. I told him I wasn't hungry, so he made me up a plate of leftover food for me to collect that afternoon instead.

I survived nearly an hour before making my excuses and leaving. I hated being the first to go and drawing attention to myself; trying to meet everyone's eye as I said goodbye. I drove home and wept, knowing full well I would have to pull myself together again to see my parents and collect the food my dad had so kindly saved for me. I didn't want to do this. I just wanted to be alone; but I felt that leaving early had upset them enough already.

I managed another hour or so at their house later, before finally being able to retreat to the quiet with only the rabbits for company. I was gutted: for letting my parents down when they wanted me fully present; for not sticking to my own resolution to leave to help my mental stability; for my illness making me concentrate more on myself and on trying to remain calm, and therefore drawing my focus away from what the day was really supposed to be about. I felt selfish and grief-stricken and very, very sad.

Two days later, I was back in the control room for a second visit, as promised. The commute was surprisingly manageable, which I believe was largely attributable to my "field trip" with Daniel. Driving that same stretch of road was much less traumatic than stopping and absorbing it. I shed a few tears there and back, and was jittery once I'd stopped driving at the end of my journeys, but I was safe and in control, with absolutely no flashbacks. The visit itself was on a busier day than my earlier one. Still no RTCs during the short time I was there – for which I felt grateful and frustrated in equal measure, keen to avoid them, yet also wanting to test myself – but at one point, duplicate calls were being received for a particular incident. The 9s ringing in simultaneously overwhelmed me rather, and I was anxious and on edge for the whole of my visit. But I survived without having to leave the room.

I had my next session with Therapist Lady a couple of days after that and we had a lot to discuss. In the fortnight between sessions, I had visited Control twice, had had two emotional talks with Jon, had attended a funeral, and had had a breakdown on the side of the A34. I was worried she might think I'd taken on too much, too soon; certainly discussing the events with friends afterwards gave me that impression. Richard was concerned I might have set myself back by facing something as brutal as visiting the crash site. He thought perhaps I should have waited until I was in a better head space and had finished with my therapy. I'd figured that, as I was already off sick, what more harm could it do? I was already exposing myself through Control visits, therapy sessions and talking in depth with Jon. Admittedly, I hadn't expected my reaction on the A34 to be quite as vicious as it was but I didn't believe it to have been detrimental. Fortunately, Therapist Lady agreed with me. She would have preferred to have known about my actions beforehand so we could have prepared (whoops!) but, as I was due to drive that route anyway, it made sense to face it with a friend first. She also agreed that, if I felt well enough to try to go back to work on a slow-phased return, it was probably the right time to do so.

I didn't know if I felt well enough or not – but by that point, I hated being off sick more than ever. I also knew I'd stabilised somewhat and that the next logical step forwards was to face my fear and try to return. The last busy couple of weeks had boosted my morale a little: I was making strides in my recovery and I felt some pride in having endured the exposure I'd had so far.

I had an Occupational Health telephone appointment the day before my sickness ended and we ran through how I was doing and what I needed going forward. The lady I spoke to was very accommodating and agreed my first couple of tours should be day shifts only, for just four hours, and with no plugging-in of my headset. That way, I could be totally focused on absorbing my working environment while limiting my exposure at the same time. We agreed that a plan would be locally agreed with my line manager; something flexible according to progress made.

CHAPTER 14
FIT

I booked fit that afternoon, Wednesday 6th April. I repeated my actions from three months ago and texted a colleague to book me fit discreetly. I would inform my managers direct anyway, and I didn't want the gamble of having to explain my situation to whoever happened to pick up the phone; that was more than I could handle.

Booking fit also meant I was able to reach out to Junior Citizens once more. They hadn't been running since the beginning of the pandemic, but were finally launching again and had schools booked in – coincidentally starting that same week when I was returning to work. I'd popped in the day before to have a chat with the person now running it (it had changed hands since Joseph's role had been altered during Covid) and I explained my situation. Jack was the watch manager now in charge and I'd known him for many years since being a cadet as a teenager. He was happy to let me come in if I was well enough, and to shadow another instructor until I got the feel of it. So, the day after booking fit, I attended JCs for the first time in two years.

I was terrified. I knew how the safety centre ran inside out; knew how to deliver scenarios; knew everything like the back of my hand. Yet, the idea of instructing a bunch of kids was daunting. Talking to staff and engaging in conversation was stressful and felt pressured. The fact that I was once again in a fire station, and knowing what that meant from my experience the week prior, left me extremely hypervigilant and tense. I found the noise of the children and the interactive scenarios overwhelming and just too much. To add more strain to my nerves, Jack was learning on the job – not his fault at all, but he was trying to figure things out and needed guidance, not hindrance from a wobbly person like me. There was also a shortage of staff, so all this added up, leaving me a shaky, fearful mess. I tried to describe how I was feeling to Jack and ended up bursting into tears. He was very kind and, misunderstanding me, printed off a cheat-sheet full of notes for the scenario I was to do. I explained to him with Sasha's help – thankfully, she was also instructing that day – that I knew what to say; it was ingrained in my brain after having done it for many years. It was the total overwhelm and hypervigilance that was messing with my head.

I ended up buddying with Jack to instruct one of the scenarios but I didn't speak to the kids for the whole morning; trying to settle myself and acclimatising back into the role; trying to still the panic and palpitations I was experiencing. When the bells went down repeatedly – which I knew they would at some point as my luck seemed to work like that! – I reacted very similarly to how I had done before. I was able to excuse myself. Then I'd run out to the balcony for fresh air and stand there shaking, letting the flashbacks wash over me, until my body and my mind regained control. Another member of staff, Ethan, was a fabulous support and I could confide in him. He was extremely concerned about my reaction but realised I had to sort myself out; he couldn't fix it. So, he'd wait next to me with a cup of tea until I came to.

By the afternoon, I'd settled enough to take some of the teaching from Jack and deliver it myself. I realised, though, that I wasn't able to instruct by myself – if the station turned out mid-scenario, it wasn't safe or professional to leave a group of ten-year-olds unattended. So we came up with a plan: where staffing permitted it, I would always buddy with someone; when we were short, Ethan would relieve me of my teaching duties when required. His role was more behind-the-scenes, not child-facing, and I was able to swap positions with him and do what I needed to do to calm down in private before taking back over. For me, this was another box ticked. JCs was something I had desperately missed since the pandemic and I was glad to be back in some capacity. Even so, I was disappointed and infuriated with myself for reacting and being triggered so strongly in a job I'd been comfortable with for fourteen years. This had once been one of my safe spaces to retire to – yet clearly I was struggling to even be present there. Surely my trauma therapy should have mended this by now? As it was, I felt more vulnerable and nowhere near to being fixed.

I returned to work on Saturday 9th April. I was only to work for four hours, and had been invited by Jon to call into the station for a cuppa with him afterwards. The shift progressed as well as it could have done; I was anxious, hypervigilant, scared, but there were no RTCs in the short weekend hours I was in for, and I remained within the room for the duration. I cried on my journey in and back again but that was expected and nothing new.

I had a meeting with Debbie, who was very considerate over what needed to be done. She understood my reservations but was also firm on making strides forward. We drew up a schedule between us on Occupational Health's recommendation and drafted the next nine tours, with the aim by the end of my being on full hours and full duties. I would be supernumerary for six of them, which was a relief. Somehow, knowing I wasn't expected to participate released some of the pressure: I knew I could leave the room if it got too much, and I had legitimate approval to do so. Not that anybody would have said anything – my watch were still very supportive of my recovery – but it made it easier to accept in my own mind.

Another colleague was also rejoining the workplace from sick leave after a bout of Long Covid, so it was nice to be "newbies" together. I survived my first shift and spoke to Jon about it at length, but I couldn't help feeling slightly disappointed I had no RTCs coming in to test myself with. I would never wish ill on anyone, but facing collisions was the only way to aid my recovery.

The next day was similar to the first. I was very aware that I only had two tours – four short shifts in total with my restrictions – before I was expected to plug in my headset and try for some admin lines and radio messages in the secondary position. This scared me, so I tried to make every minute count when I was at work. I found myself still anxious and jittery whenever the phone rang, and I monitored the screens of my colleagues when calls were being received, almost to brace myself. I was exhausted when I got home after each shift – a combination of poor sleep and riding a constant feeling of being in flight mode the whole time I was in Control, ready to tip over the edge at any point. That consistent flood of adrenaline was shattering and I found myself napping back at home once a shift was finished.

The second tour, again, was similar to the first. Weekends tend generally to be calmer, and with no commuters the numbers of RTCs are more likely to drop significantly. My first two weeks back coincided with weekends and the Easter Bank Holiday, so I was given a false sense of security in two ways: the calls weren't a true reflection of the average day, and the roads for my commute were generally clear. I had a further CBT session with Therapist Lady, but there wasn't much new ground to cover as my work shifts so far had been uneventful. We agreed to meet again virtually after my next tour, by which time I would have done more hours, more shifts, and on busier days.

I returned to work the following week, this time expecting to do five hours on my day shifts and three hours in the evening of my nights. My first day was the Monday morning after Easter week, when schools were back in and traffic was at full capacity. I was scheduled to plug in and take calls and messages, albeit not 9s. I was also to be monitored by my crew manager when undertaking my additional roles, which seemed a good level of support to me.

I got to work that morning extremely stressed out and overwhelmed, close to tears from the worst journey I had driven in a long time. I sat in the designated secondary radio position and logged in ready to commence my duties. I felt as though I'd vomit if I opened my mouth – I don't know how I wasn't sick from the stress I was feeling and apparently I was a very funny colour for most of the day. I couldn't speak to anyone or look anyone in the eye; I felt incredibly vulnerable and somehow exposed; waiting for the world to collapse in, for a call to end in catastrophe. I wanted to run, abandon my seat and just leave the whole situation as flight mode threatened to overwhelm me, but I knew I had to be stubborn and find the strength to see this through. Then, finally, what I had avoided for the entirety of my observing shifts happened – we received reports of a collision.

My reaction was instant and extreme. Shock, horror, panic, dread all rose up inside me and I could do nothing but sit at my desk with my head in my hands and just *feel*, trying to absorb what was coursing through my whole being. It was terrifying; I was shaking, tears silently streaming; my hands were unconsciously running through my hair, gripping my head in an attempt to grasp the flashbacks that were pulling me out of reality. Once again, I had that odd, horrifying sensation that there was something acting as a block on my brain and preventing me from doing anything except receive the onslaught. Everyone around me faded into nothing. I noticed no one, full only of my own senses, until things started to quieten and I was finally able to sit my head back up as hell relented.

I knew what it was I was experiencing; I knew that my almighty trigger wasn't the new RTC, but the fact it sent me flying back to the original one. I was left weak, drained and shaky, but I remained in the room to try to deal with it. It was interesting, as well, to note the flashbacks seemed to convert my response from flight mode, to freezing: the intensity of everything washing over me meant I could do nothing but be still and ride it out.

I returned to work the following day feeling a little more prepared for what was to come – or so I thought. The 9s were busy, ringing constantly, and I struggled with the persistent noise seeming to drill into my eardrums.

Until all of a sudden, it stopped: nothing.

The unpredictability of emergency calls means there are busy spells and lulls intermittently. But I was then triggered, freaked out by the weight of silence on my overwrought senses. I wasn't sure if I'd just reached my limit over the last couple of days; or whether the silence was overly loud in my hypervigilant brain; or if my anxiety was shooting through the roof in anticipation of calls coming in … but I knew I wasn't expected to have a breakdown over nothing. Once again, I sat shaking at my desk, full of horror, until Clara pulled me out of the room, calmed me down and made me a cup of tea. I spent an extra hour sitting in the restroom, stilling my nerves, before I felt ready to drive home after my shift. I felt like an utter failure – and embarrassed to have broken down over nothing.

So, this was my reaction?! Three months of sickness, weeks and weeks of reliving therapy, trying to endure everything PTSD had thrown at me since August – for me to go to pieces regardless? That in itself was disheartening; frightening. But suddenly, everything felt threatened. If I couldn't figure out a way to manage this, there was no way I could continue in my job. Work had been patient a long time but where does a line have to be drawn?

I'm a very logical thinker: things need to be clear and explained to me; reasons provided. I was in a way grateful that my PTSD manifested in physical symptoms that I could use to reason with my own brain. However, this latest reaction defied reason. It was illogical and scary and it worried me greatly.

I tried to rest on my return home but I couldn't sleep. My mind was whirring at top speed, I was overcome with terrible thoughts that wouldn't settle down and my stomach was churning. Clara had already checked in on me after that afternoon. When I still felt terrible hours later, I reached out further, messaging Daniel and Jon on our group chat, and messaging Richard too. Jon offered support and was sure I was still making baby steps in the right direction; Daniel informed me that he'd spoken to Keith, who had witnessed my last couple of shifts at work and felt optimistic and confident that my reactions were more under control and not lasting for as long as they had done before I'd booked sick. It was reassuring that he felt so positive about my progress, but inside I felt my reactions were more intense and therefore burning themselves out more quickly.

Richard was very straight-talking as always, which I appreciated. He told me to talk it through with Therapist Lady as I might actually find it was part of the process and of making progress. But he added that if it was too much, then I should book sick again: no job was worth becoming ill over. He said to try not to become consumed with worry about it until I'd spoken to her, but to also perhaps start thinking about a Plan B in terms of career – or at least coming to terms with the possibility of needing a Plan B. He gave me a good analogy, too, of the whole process being like a rollercoaster: right now I was riding in a dip, about to come back up. That made sense; except I felt I was so far into that dip that I was falling out of the carriage.

Richard's wise words may have been practical but I didn't like them. The prospect of having to find a new job was scary. It also meant, in my eyes at least, that I would have failed.

I decided to ground myself more permanently – in tattoo form. This was something I'd been considering for a while. I'd never had a tattoo before but only because, for me, it needed to have a lot of meaning to be forever etched into my skin. I decided to have something to symbolise my diagnosis and my journey, both to keep me tethered to the here and now when I was triggered, and as a reminder to myself to keep going. I chose a peacock. My natural affinity with these birds had come about from that rental flat, so many years ago now, and the free-roaming birds that resided there. They were proud and stubborn; unapologetic, daring and beautiful. A peacock feather also symbolises regrowth, which I felt perfectly reflected my situation. I love colour and vibrancy, and a peacock in tattoo form seemed ideal for that. The bird itself is situated on my left forearm, on the underside; it stares at me with a firm, piercing eye that I can gaze on when I'm trying to calm myself. The head and body are coloured in pinks and purples, feminine and striking; the tail feathers are blues and greens, with a vivid teal lending a nod to the PTSD awareness ribbon. I also had the ribbon detailed behind the peacock, rippling in the wind. It was a stark reminder to me to push through whatever I was experiencing at the time, and to understand in the moment why I would be feeling what I was feeling.

CHAPTER 15
EMDR

My next session with Therapist Lady came as quite a shock to me. After describing my previous shifts and how I'd been triggered, she seemed pretty stumped for answers. She believed that perhaps we had done all we could with Trauma CBT and that it hadn't worked. She suggested I see how things progressed over the next few weeks, as there was still a chance I might settle down and reactions would lessen as time went on; but she thought it highly likely she had reached the end of being able to help me. She suggested I might benefit from something called EMDR therapy; said she would speak to a colleague about it but that it was likely I'd have to be re-referred through Talking Therapies. The waiting list for EMDR was a long one due to it being specialised – there were only two people in the whole county under the NHS who were qualified to deliver this specific type of therapy.

Because of this, the waiting times were likely to exceed ten months, if they deemed me eligible. Her advice was to go back to Keith instead, as he had previously mentioned that further options may be available.

I was winded with this news. After nearly twenty allotted, trauma-specific therapy sessions, I was deemed still broken? There was no way I could withstand a wait of nearly another year for more help, and I had no reason to believe my employment would be that patient either. I had no clue what EMDR was, although I knew Keith had – he'd mentioned it briefly in one of our conversations. So, I set about both educating myself and talking to him the next shift I was in work. From what I could glean on the internet, EMDR was *the* treatment for PTSD specifically, and seemed to work wonders for those who had tried it. It stood for Eye Movement Desensitisation and Reprocessing therapy. It seemed to involve mimicking the state of REM sleep, with therapists moving fingers or lights, or tapping bilaterally, to help patients process stuck memories that the brain had been unable to deal with due to trauma. The end result was to reduce the intensity and vivacity of traumatic memories; not dispense with them but just remove the distress associated with them. It all sounded very clever and magical to me and, quite frankly, I was keen to give anything a go. This felt like my last chance: if this PTSD-specific treatment did not work, then I figured I was out of options.

I was incredibly grateful and relieved when, on speaking to Keith, he was totally on board with this plan. He had to speak to various departments at work and to higher-ranking officers to gain approval, but he was confident that the brigade could support me financially and provide this specific type of therapy through private means, after assessment by both an EMDR specialist and Occupational Health. I later got an email from a lady in HR, who had been assisting Keith with this on my behalf; it detailed the exact stipulations of this agreement. I was to be assessed, which the brigade would kindly fund; if eligible, I would be responsible for paying the tax on my therapy sessions, as it was considered a benefit in kind. The brigade would have to review the recommendations from my assessment and would then consider funding a number of sessions. They also advised I was to remain in touch with my GP and current therapist, as appropriate. I agreed to all of this, and awaited further contact for assessment.

The following week at work was my hardest yet. The schedule drawn up between myself and Debbie seemed to be gathering pace: now, at the beginning of May, I was due to attempt to take some 9s calls. The first day of the tour, I was positioned on radio, easing myself back into the working week. At this point I was working six-hour days and four-hour evenings on the night shifts. It was exhausting, mainly due to being on edge and tensed up for a prolonged period of time. My body was prepared to react to danger at the drop of a hat and, combined with little sleep, I was finding myself once again napping on lunch breaks, absolutely shattered.

I came in on my second day, shaking from head to toe. I seated myself in the secondary 9s position, with Marcus strategically placed at the desk behind me as the crew manager supporting me. As I logged in to the computer, I was unable to look at anyone; trying to choke down impulses to both cry and vomit; trying to act like a rational person. My fear was on another level: terror, absolute sheer terror consumed me. I was petrified. I was also frustrated with myself: I knew the job. I was good at answering 999 calls. It wouldn't make any impact on the caller's situation if I took the conversation or one of my colleagues did. Yet, I knew my reactions were worse when sitting in these positions. That's why I'd adapted my role to avoid them so many months ago. If I spoke to the caller, there was no thinking time, no adjustment, no pause to let my mind try to catch up, or for me to straighten my thoughts. I would have to push everything aside to deal with the emergency, knowing it would come back twofold once I'd hung up the line. I'd be plunged straight into flashbacks, and I knew that each time I was triggered, that family died for me again. I also knew that the possibility of further catastrophe could only be one phone call away. It was a distressing task for me in both ways; taking 999 calls, in my mind, brought the past instantly back to the present moment, and also had the real potential to repeat itself once more.

Marcus spoke to me; asked if I was logged in and ready. I couldn't look at him. I just told him, no, I wasn't ready yet. My voice caught and died at the end of that sentence and he knew. He told me to take as much time as I needed. Debbie wasn't yet in the room – she was in a meeting with Sam. When she reappeared about thirty minutes later, I still sat there, motionless, the occasional tear sliding down my face as I desperately tried to maintain composure. She looked directly at me as she entered the room and asked if I was ok – that was the tipping point. I cried. Big, ugly sobs like a child, to the extent that I was hyperventilating. I absolutely broke down, so she pulled me from my seat and into the office next door. I cried and I cried, scared out of my wits. I couldn't have a coherent conversation at that point. She left to fetch me some tissues and a tea, and on her way out had obviously popped her head into Sam's office and said something. Sam appeared and took in the state of me. She struggled to get words from me for a good while until my panic started to ebb.

Sam's reaction was similar to Jack's when I'd been tearful in the face of a JCs scenario those few weeks ago. She kindly but firmly suggested I do some practice calls, using the training system and calls put in by her in the next room. She assumed I was daunted, anxious about taking a 9s call after so long. Her solutions were from a good place but misguided and totally off the mark. I tried to explain to her and to Debbie; tried to put my scrambled thoughts into words: it wasn't the act of taking a call that I was scared of, just as with the scenario at JCs. I knew how to do my job and to do it well. The overwhelm and the terror arose from the implications of particular calls I could end up taking. My body was stressed out to its maximum, knowing that RTCs were at some point a certainty; and when they came around, I knew the world would end again for me, over and over, and I would hear those vehicles crash once more. I also knew the real potential for people to be killed, just as they had been in the past. Fake calls didn't remove that possibility.

Debbie and Sam convinced me I needed a breather. They asked Marcus to take me out for a walk to calm me down. But Sam also laid it out that she wanted me to take a 9s call by the time I was done that day, or we would be doing practice calls together instead.

I went on a long walk with Marcus. Behind our workplace is a footpath that leads up and out of the town, surrounded by fields and countryside. This was a perfect place to gain clarity. Marcus chatted a lot to begin with, calming me down with talk of his own experiences. I was able to speak more fluently once we'd reached the top of the hill. We spent a while taking in the surroundings, me trying to straighten out my mind. He was a star – patient and humouring me with my crazy, racing thoughts, but also understanding me and my severe reaction. We were out for a good couple of hours in the end. I felt a little guilty about that – tying up both of us and preventing us from doing our jobs – but we'd left on the station manager's insistence and I figured I wouldn't be much use if I returned too early anyway.

By the time I'd calmed down and we'd walked back to work, I had hardened my resolve in my mind. I would not be conducting practice calls with Sam; I refused to be treated as a newcomer, or incompetent. I was still terrified but my stubborn mind knew this was a hurdle I somehow had to overcome. If I couldn't pass this test – if I couldn't take emergency calls – then my job was as good as finished. So I told myself to put on a brave face and do it anyway; to "man up" – not a phrase I would ever use to anyone else, particularly those struggling with mental health issues, but that didn't seem to prevent me from saying it to myself.

We returned to the control room. I was slightly embarrassed to face my colleagues again but also defiant, despite my meltdown. They were all supportive in any case, as they had been all along. I sat in my seat, gearing myself up to answer the phone; still as fearful as ever but thankfully having cried myself dry. I was shaking like a leaf. About an hour of this passed, with me rooted to my chair, before I spotted my opportunity: my gateway into answering the phone. We often receive calls from alarm receiving centres and carelines – still emergency calls, but filtered and rung through by a member of their staff. The calls ring on a slightly different number that con-ops can recognise. I saw one come in and, making a split-second decision, I answered it. I knew there would be no crashes involved and that the call had already been filtered to an extent. As far as Debbie and Sam were concerned, I was now answering calls. In my own mind, it was a way of easing myself in gently. I didn't acknowledge the call once I'd hung up the line. When I caught Marcus's eye, he nodded and smiled in encouragement, but otherwise I didn't look at my colleagues or address the enormity of what I'd just done. I took a few more calls in the same vein, picking and choosing, until I was brave enough to answer a proper 9s towards the end of my shift which, thankfully, was uneventful.

My night shifts continued in the same fashion. I was asked – expected – to sit in the secondary 9s position for both short shifts. Each time I could have said something to Debbie and backed out – nobody, I'm sure, would have questioned it –but I was determined to push through. That was the definition of being brave, wasn't it? Being scared and doing it anyway. I didn't feel brave at all but I wanted to be that person; I needed to try. PTSD wouldn't beat me so I tried to be the con-op I desperately wanted to return to being: someone confident and able to do their job. It was still terrifying on an insane scale. I found myself focusing on the person in front of me on primary 9s and panicking internally when they stepped away from their desk, or were busy on another call, leaving me directly in the firing line for the phone ringing. My stress levels were elevated to such an extent that, during both shifts, I ended up excusing myself to the toilets to vomit.

I realised at the end of my tour that, for the entirety of my four days, I hadn't eaten an actual meal. I'd had picky bits in between – I was obviously in no danger of starving – but I couldn't eat at work as the stress would make me bring it back up. I often wasn't very hungry after each shift; just wiped out at the end of another brutal day. My wellbeing seemed to wax and wane: on my days off, I would catch up on nourishment and rest; between shifts, not a lot of sleeping or eating was really happening. I was also still surviving on antihistamines to cope with stress levels and associated allergic reactions.

The following tour was similar. I got a brief respite on my days as we were relocated to our Secondary Control, due to some maintenance work taking place in the control room, so I was scheduled to be on radio positions. Even then, I was forced to answer a 9s call at one point when there was no one else available in the room. My luck, of course, ensured that this happened to be an RTC, although fortunately a minor one. I dealt with the call, left the room triggered, and rode out my reaction until I was stable enough to rejoin the watch. All I could do was hold out for the end of the week; I had some leave to take and was due to have nearly a fortnight off, which my nerves desperately needed. I was also due to have a scheduled assessment from an EMDR practitioner.

My night shifts stepped up a gear before I took my leave: my hours upped again, this time so I was working six and a half hours each evening and finishing at 01:00hrs. This, weirdly, suited me – the commute was less pressurised with no other cars on the roads at that time in the morning. The shifts also saw me finally sitting in the primary 9s position, five weeks after returning to work. It was horrendous. I was shaking and tearful again; I was sick several times; and at one point Debbie walked over to me, trying not to cry at my desk, and just hugged me. It must have shown in my face what tough going this was for me. I knew I was committed at this point – to take my foot off the pedal, to book sick again as some suggested to me, would only land me back at square one when it came to returning again. I needed to ride this experience out and hope it would get easier. I did take some RTC calls on these shifts – being on primary 9s for a longer period meant that was almost guaranteed – and I managed to remain in the room as I absorbed my reaction, sitting at my desk with my head in my hands once the call was done, trembling and reliving everything. I tried not to escape out of the room onto the balcony, although quite often I would retreat out there afterwards to regain some composure. But I was really doing my best to remain in the control room for the most part, resisting the scream of my nerves to flee. When triggered, my body would continue to freeze with flashbacks and I would sit there, fighting for control.

I caught up with Sam too, before going on leave. I tried to explain the situation to her, and used the words I was telling myself: that I needed to get a grip, to man up and deal with what I was experiencing. She, to my dismay, agreed and told me I needed to "wear my big girl pants" to get through this period of progression. I learnt from that conversation: because I'd used that throwaway phrase of telling myself to get a grip, I'd inadvertently given the impression that I wasn't already putting in every single fibre of effort to progress. I felt a little as though I'd done myself a disservice, with her responding comment having stemmed from my own. So since then, although I've continued to push with all my determination and grit to succeed, I've also tried to be kinder to myself, especially when I've felt I'm struggling. Putting your "big girl pants on" was a well-used phrase with Sam. It didn't have any malice behind it and her response was initiated by me. But it struck a chord and reverberated around my brain. It taught me another lesson: I would never have directed the words I used to someone else, so perhaps I needed to refrain from using them to myself too.

The EMDR assessment was conducted via video call that same week by a psychologist who lived many miles away from me, but who worked for the company the brigade had sourced. I talked through everything with her: my experiences leading to my PTSD and what I'd covered in my Trauma CBT sessions. She seemed confident they would be able to assist me and explained that my treatment so far seemed to have desensitised me, but hadn't enabled me to process my trauma – hence why I was still reacting so strongly. I was relieved she appeared so optimistic that EMDR could help; that I hadn't reached the end of the road yet.

I asked to have these new sessions conducted in person, rather than virtually. The psychologist would type up her assessment report so work could consider if they were happy to pay. Then, all being well, I would be able to start my next course of treatment. I kept my fingers crossed.

CHAPTER 16
SURFING

Time marched on and I found myself in yet another form of limbo, waiting for things to progress. My leave was spent recuperating and continuing to push myself out there socially. I still couldn't handle busy crowds or loud noises very well, but I did my best, despite my hypervigilance, to maintain a normal-ish lifestyle and distract myself from my continually racing thoughts. I had a further session with Therapist Lady. However, we were winding down now that we'd reached the end and I was waiting for EMDR to start; there wasn't a lot more to say. I had a couple more sessions at JCs, which, to my dismay, didn't seem to show much improvement either. I still relied heavily on colleagues to take over my group if I became overwhelmed, and I continued to be severely triggered by the turnouts of the fire station. My hours increased, week by week, on returning to work from my leave but, thankfully, I was

161

still not being counted towards the crewing levels until my duties were back up to full capacity. I fought with myself every day to maintain control of my reactions, yet my triggering seemed as severe as it ever had been.

The assessment report from the EMDR assessor came back confirming that treatment would be beneficial. It stated: "It seems that while she has desensitised to some of the traumatic components of her memories through reliving work, she has not fully processed the memories and continues to experience significant somatic, emotional, and cognitive symptoms at work when required to handle 999 calls." The assessor's recommendation was to enrol on eight to twelve sessions of EMDR. I was relieved that the report reflected exactly how I was feeling, and grateful that my workplace took it seriously enough to address that. Finance for the sessions was agreed; Occupational Health were kept informed and I had another appointment with them. Then, I found myself waiting for a start date as the company sought an EMDR practitioner who was within travelling distance, so that I could undertake face-to-face sessions.

In the meantime, I was sent a link from Clara regarding a pilot scheme being run by the Fire Fighters Charity. The first of its kind, this trial, three-day course was specifically for beneficiaries who were suffering from trauma. It was based at Harcombe House but run in conjunction with a police welfare scheme known as Surfwell, also based in Devon. Surfwell uses surf therapy to help those from the emergency services deal with mental health struggles. It sounded fantastic, and more targeted to my needs than my previous spell at the charity had been. I requested the time off and, to my surprise, Sam readily agreed, on the condition that Therapist Lady didn't think it would be detrimental to my ongoing treatment. I emailed her and, with her blessing, contacted the charity to book my place on the course.

I set off for Devon after my day shift on 12th June 2022. This time, I was a little more confident, knowing what I was heading towards, and I felt a mixture of excitement and anticipation. I knew that the next few days were going to be hard and emotionally draining.

I arrived at the charity later than most, having had to work the shift beforehand, and was directed this time to a bungalow that I would be sharing with another course participant. We hit it off almost immediately – it was nice to make a friend straight away and good to have a living space with shared areas.

The course was programmed in a similar way to my first visit: a measured mixture of workshops, walks and activities such as yoga. This time, though, they were all focused on trauma. There were six of us enrolled, serving and non-serving personnel, but all with a traumatic story that was impinging greatly on our current wellbeing. The workshops were incredible and on point, talking about what trauma is, how it affected our bodies and our minds, and what tools we could use to assist us. We ran through symptoms and how they could affect our relationships with others, and talked about how PTSD develops by trauma becoming "trapped". We discussed setting boundaries and understanding change, and had a whole workshop on post-traumatic growth, including the recommended treatments for PTSD, and undertaking self-compassion. I was absolutely blown away by how powerful these classroom sessions were for me. They were, in a way, a form of group therapy. We all bonded quickly and I felt trusting enough to be open about my whole journey, knowing that everybody in the room had experienced something similar – they got it.

We all cried at various points – I found the workshop on post-traumatic growth particularly difficult to talk through. Everything felt very raw to me. I was in the middle of my therapy, CBT had failed me and I was relying wholly on EMDR to work its magic. Every symptom we talked through I could recognise in myself; it was like a slap in the face to know just how far I still had to go, with so much resting on this therapy. A couple of the group had had EMDR and gave it positive reviews. Yet they were both here, sitting alongside me, still struggling with trauma. Where would I be afterwards?

Monday and Wednesday were based at Harcombe, and I quickly fell back into the routine of their scheduled sessions, mealtimes, then a few drinks in the evening with my new friends. I found these evening discussions equally valuable, debriefing on the heavy sessions of the day – often, more tears were shed.

Tuesday was a little different, as this was the day we would be at the beach undertaking a Surfwell course run by the police. We had an early start, having to meet at a beach approximately an hour away from Harcombe House. The plan was to split ourselves between two vehicles. I sat in the back seat of one car with two others – and realised shortly after we'd set off that I couldn't tolerate being in a carpool. I'd never been a nervous passenger and, so far, had solidly refused to let my fears deter me from driving – but I hadn't been in a vehicle with multiple passengers since my diagnosis. Being in the back seat in a car full of people, travelling on a road that was clearly a busy route for lorries first thing in the morning, sent my senses screaming. I tried to keep a lid on it but by the time the journey had ended, I was a shaky, teary mess. The other occupants of my vehicle were considerate and understanding, but I was shocked and infuriated at my own reaction. I had had no reason to suspect the journey might be an issue – I'd been driven by Daniel to Control and back, and to the A34 for our field trip, so why my severe reaction now? The fact that, if the vehicle collided, it meant a whole car full of us would be affected seemed to be the differing factor.

The time with Surfwell was nothing short of incredible. It was aimed at emergency services personnel and run by serving police officers, all of whom had suffered from mental health issues and trauma themselves. We started the day in a bit of a circle, with each member of staff introducing themselves and telling their story. Afterwards, we were paired up one-to-one with our allocated instructors, who each took us down to the beach to give us a morning's introductory lesson in surfing. There was something magical about playing in the cold water with a surfboard, and the personal contact with individuals after the classroom introductions meant that talking seemed natural; it came easily. I was an open book with my partner, who asked all the right questions to allow me to explain exactly what had brought me to them that day. It was a relief again to be able to speak to someone who understood what I was talking about and could absolutely relate.

The surfing itself was exhilarating. It was the first time in nearly a year when I'd had real fun and forgotten everything else in my head. I had big adrenaline rushes but this time for the right reasons, and I was able to burn them off the way bodies are supposed to. I certainly didn't display any actual skill in surfing (I had a feeling I wouldn't – I'm far too clumsy!) but my instructor described me as fearless: I gave every suggestion a go, loving the thrill as I picked up speed each time.

After lunch all together at a nearby beach café, we retreated back to the building where we'd started and each had a proper one-to-one discussion with the police officer we were partnered with. My conversation was heavy going but so valuable. I was asked about my current state of mind; if I had any thoughts of self-harm or suicide. I was struck by how compassionate each of the Surfwell personnel were; they made sure we felt safe as we were talking. I explained how I was pinning everything on the imminent EMDR sessions and how the thought of them failing left me with a sense of hopelessness. I talked about how I was feeling and my struggles with each day – not to the point of suicidal thoughts but not being in a good place. I found my partner had that similar, brutally honest way about him that I'd often admired in Richard – and he mirrored Richard's opinion that it wouldn't hurt to consider another career as a backup should the therapy not yield the results I hoped for. His own traumatic experiences within his policing role had led him to a redeployment for similar reasons and he could resonate with that struggle. He also advised taking up a low-intensity activity or exercise that I could do regularly; something to mimic the endorphins I'd got from the surfing that day. Interestingly, he picked up on my turn of phrase when describing myself: I'd referred to myself as stubborn and obstinate in fighting my PTSD, using what he perceived to be negative words for positive characteristics in my personality. He described me as strong, determined and brave, which he said was evidenced by how I'd pushed myself through some very difficult situations. I was quite humbled and touched by this – a stranger, someone who'd known me for only a day, had picked up on some of the qualities in my personality that I strived for but couldn't recognise in myself. He sent me a report later on, including attachments covering grounding and breathing techniques.

The next day, Harcombe House ran a workshop on the benefits of cold water, such as the sea when surfing. That's when I knew I must seriously consider my options for a new hobby, as the Surfwell instructor had discussed with me, but that it should involve water in some way. I went home from my second spell with the Fire Fighters Charity with a lot to think about, some new ideas to consider, and feeling rather wrung out on the back of an exhausting, emotional few days. The course was exactly what I had needed.

The following week, finally, things started to progress. I got a date for my first face-to-face appointment. It was to be on 28th June 2022 with an EMDR practitioner based in the city, about forty minutes from my house. I knew the first appointment would mainly be introductory content; nevertheless, I was excited that things were finally shifting again.

The day before the appointment, I met up with Clara for afternoon cocktails. We put the world to rights and, in a fairly quiet, non-overwhelming setting, I was able to let my hair down – the first time in a long, long while. I felt a lot of love and appreciation for one of many friends who had had my back in recent months. Coincidentally, our meet-up fell on what I discovered was PTSD Awareness Day. That made me think: I wanted to – needed to – extend my gratitude to those friends who had supported me. I knew deep down they didn't consider me a chore but I also knew they had put up with a lot of my drama and I wanted them to know they honestly were the ones who had got me through it so far. I never hesitated, if I was having a bad day, to message them, and they needed to know that that went a long way. The Awareness Day also made me think that perhaps there needed to be some education for those who hadn't been privy to my diagnosis and struggles. I knew, at work, that I'd kept it quiet and confidential for as long as I could – and I knew that, in doing so, I had pushed several people away. It wasn't personal to them; I just could only deal with so much without being overwhelmed and I had to focus on myself. I could anticipate certain people's reactions too, which, again, I wouldn't have been able to tolerate at the time PTSD was starting to raise its head. However, things were changing now.

As of July – my next tour at work – I would be up to full hours, full duties and no longer being counted as supernumerary personnel. I wasn't sure about this – I didn't think I was ready. There would be a lot of expectation for me to remain in the room and do my job, despite being triggered, if I was now being counted towards crewing. I knew that, practically, it wouldn't make any difference – if I had to remove myself from the situation, everybody would support me in doing so, especially as treatment was still ongoing – but it was a lot of pressure to put on myself. Nevertheless, Sam and Debbie wanted me to try; so I would try. If it backfired, they would have to re-evaluate my supernumerary position.

I felt, though, that the time had come to tell people what I'd been going through. I was bolstered by both my recent trip to the Fire Fighters Charity and my imminent start with EMDR; I felt I needed to be honest and explain to people in my life why I'd been acting the way I had. I would be coming into contact with more people at work now my hours had been restored, especially if colleagues worked overtime on my watch. I wanted them to know why I might be triggered, what that would look like and how to react around me when it happened. I didn't want to be avoided or talked about behind my back; I didn't want any stigma to be attached to my illness. I wanted people to know they could approach me and ask questions. So, I wrote a social media post relating to PTSD Awareness Day and explained, without going into full details, what my story was. It was out in the open then. Everybody else would now know, particularly at work, that it wasn't a secret anymore; it was something I was happy to talk about and wanted to educate people in.

Writing something for all to see was scary, daunting and emotional – but I'm so glad I did it. Apart from the public comments of support, I also had people private messaging me, talking to me about it and asking questions. I'm happy I was able to initiate this and knew that from now on, if progress was to continue, both with my welfare and in helping others, then I needed to keep talking.

CHAPTER 17
MAGIC LADY

I attended my first EMDR session the next day. The lady seemed nice; friendly but professional, with many years of experience behind her. We didn't start on EMDR straight away, as I'd predicted. This was an introductory session to explain about PTSD and how EMDR would work to make things easier, and to ask me again to talk through the story of why I was there. The practitioner seemed to think it should be fairly straightforward to approach: Single Incident PTSD normally responded well to EMDR. I was relieved to hear that. We then practised some safe space imagery and grounding, as I had with CBT, and I booked in my first proper session the following week.

Back at work, conducting shifts without the safe supernumerary label was difficult. I tried to manage my triggers as they came; I did my best to remain in the room when RTCs occurred. However, it was evident to everyone that I was no good when I was zoned out and dealing with my own head. During my first shift back, I had to handle two RTCs within a short space of time of each other: with the first, I excused myself pretty quickly as we had work experience visitors in the room and I didn't want to embarrass myself and be triggered in front of them. I chose instead to act on my screaming instincts to remove myself from the room, so that I could hyperventilate and shake on the balcony outside. The second RTC forced me to stay on the phone. The caller described the scene in front of her: a male dragging a drunk driver out of a car that had overturned and caught fire. I remained on the line with her, advising, and assessing the situation for the oncoming crews, while trying to keep overwhelming flashbacks at bay. I had to stay professional until I could collapse into a shaky, traumatised mess on my desk as soon as I'd hung up the line. The week continued in a similar fashion – even when I remained in the room when triggered, I was voiceless and wide-eyed in fear; frozen; unable to pick up a ringing phone, which forced anybody on their break to be recalled to the room to answer instead.

My supernumerary status was reinstated the following week. I was deeply humbled to discover that no fewer than five managers had all spoken up on my behalf, without my knowledge, to say I was being rushed when I clearly wasn't ready. I was put back as a supernumerary employee for an indefinite amount of time, which I felt gave me more breathing space to work through what I needed to do. I could tell, though, that Sam was keen to have me as a functioning member of staff as soon as possible. All I could do was continue to pin my hopes on EMDR.

I'd scheduled my first "proper" EMDR session as an evening appointment – being halfway between my workplace and home, it made sense to incorporate it into my commute. We sat down and the practitioner positioned herself opposite me, within touching distance but slightly to the side. She asked me to think of a particular part of my trauma memory that I seemed to have the most trouble with. There were two points that stuck out in my brain from that crash. I remembered vividly the approach of the lorry as it climbed the hill at speed, and my realisation of what would happen; I also remembered the point of impact – that loud bang that seemed to haunt me and wake me from sleep – and seeing the devastation as I passed; following its progress in my wing mirror as I continued to travel.

Between us, we opted to start with the former and work chronologically. The practitioner asked me to recall that memory; replay it in my mind. As I did so, she started to move her fingers from side to side in front of me at a steady, fast pace, making my eyes move from left to right and back again. She had asked me to sit in the chair with my legs uncrossed, explaining that some people had difficulty focusing on the memory and on her fingers simultaneously. Another option, therefore, would be for her to tap my legs rhythmically to recreate the same bilateral movements. I had no problem with following her fingers, however – multitasking in that way came naturally to me with the job I do.

I thought I would struggle to actually recall the memory visually when asked to do so – the way my brain thinks tends to be less visual and more "feeling". Often I can recall images but I can't focus on them. It's like trying to hold water in my hands, images trickle away quickly. Flashbacks have always been sharper and visually clearer – as have my dreams – but even flashbacks tend to present more to me as emotional and audible experiences rather than visual ones. I've looked into this – the way the brain works fascinates me – but while some people have pure aphantasia (they can't form mental images), I, instead, have some visual memory but on a lower scale. I was concerned this might hinder my progress and was preparing myself to try to explain to the EMDR therapist that a varied approach might be necessary. Yet, to my surprise, I didn't struggle at all, as recalling my memory while she worked on it almost seemed to hold it in the forefront of my mind. It also brought back the feelings and emotions attached to the memory, which she worked on too.

She stopped frequently after every set of finger-moving to ask what I noticed. It could be a thought, a feeling, a physical reaction, a change to the memory. I would describe to her what I was thinking; she would tell me to notice that and, without further words, she would begin again.

As I sat in the armchair, I realised my whole body was shaking; trembling. Actively recalling the memory so strongly was bringing out the somatic symptoms I would have when triggered: I was sweating; my heart thudded hard and fast. My breathing, weirdly, stopped. I seemed to hold my breath the whole time and the practitioner had to keep reminding me to breathe. My whole being was tensed, every muscle taut, my thighs cramping. After some time, I realised I was actually bracing my body for impact. My muscles were held tightly, waiting for a collision as I watched that lorry climb the hill. I also realised my feet were pressing hard into the floor. They almost hurt as I dug them into the carpet so forcefully. Eventually, I understood that I was pressing "pedals" as I sat there, trying to stop the oncoming LGV.

We kept on like this for nearly an hour. I shed a few tears and she encouraged me, with the few words she spoke between each go, to let my mind travel where it wanted to and see how things worked out. She asked how I could improve what I was seeing; how I could make the memory more bearable. By the end of the hour, recalling that lorry for me brought up a stationary vehicle on the road; a snapshot frozen in time. The image didn't change; the memory was still as it was. But if I could visualise the lorry not moving, it took away the anticipation of what would happen. This removed the fear and the anxiety of waiting for that situation to play itself out. As the image perspective altered, the practitioner's moving fingers changed pace. It was almost as though she was fixing it in place in my brain. I was blown away. I felt wrung out, drained physically and mentally, but I also experienced an odd sense of peace.

Once she'd finished, I was no longer shaking. I had let go of the tight hold on my muscles and I felt calm once more. She warned me that I would likely be processing for a couple of days afterwards, and would have vivid dreams as my head continued to work. I thanked her, set a date for the next session, then drove home. By the time I'd reached my house forty minutes later, I could feel a massive headache building. This was odd for me: I'm never one to suffer headaches but I figured it was my brain processing. As I was shattered, I headed to bed almost straight away. I slept the whole night, with the vivid dreams promised to me. When I woke up the next day, I felt just as tired. From that, I knew my brain had been processing rather than resting overnight. My whole body hurt, aching as though I'd done ten hours in the gym.

My shift at work took me by surprise. I wasn't sure how I'd be after EMDR. I had a mixture of reactions: I felt exhausted, mentally drained, and strangely vulnerable, as though my mind had been assaulted somehow. At the same time, I noticed improvements. The massive anxiety and terror I felt just being in the control room – being thrown straight into flight mode as soon as my shift began – didn't happen. *What?* I was still anxious, still jittery; my heart still leapt when the phone rang; I was still triggered by RTCs – but that crippling sense of fear, which had caused me to vomit on numerous occasions, was gone. I was so relieved, I didn't know whether to laugh or cry. I think I ended up doing both.

I had a catch-up with Marcus and explained how I'd changed seemingly overnight. An instantaneous, massive reduction in fear was nothing short of miraculous. It was like some kind of magic. I caught Richard, too, on handover and explained the same thing; he used that word as well. So, 'Magic Lady' earned her nickname. I was so utterly thankful that it had worked. Something huge had changed just from one session. The next one was booked for the following week and I waited with equal amounts of hope and dread. I hated reliving the RTC; re-experiencing it. But now I felt more certain that EMDR could help me where CBT hadn't been able to.

That session had bolstered my confidence somewhat. For the first time in what seemed like forever, I had a craving to get away and run back to my safe space – the Isle of Wight. So I booked a day trip. I drove down to Portsmouth at silly o'clock in the morning and caught the 06:00hrs ferry. I drove to a couple of viewpoints, favourite spots of mine, to watch the early morning arrive, then I headed off for breakfast at a pub, in the village where I used to live. I asked to sit in the garden overlooking the sea to eat my food. Afterwards, I spent an hour or so sitting on the beach, reading my book. I drove to a couple of tourist sites, then went on a long walk over fields and beside a lake. I finished my day at the beach once again, eating fish and chips and purchasing the biggest ice cream I could find, before listening to live music from afar and soaking in the views. My ferry home was at 23:00hrs. By the time I got back, I'd been gone a full twenty-four hours, but I felt more myself than I had in a long time.

The next week at my EMDR appointment, we worked on the second part of that crash memory: the collision itself. Magic Lady seemed satisfied that I'd responded well to our efforts the previous session. We sat again in the same position and, this time, worked through the point of impact, which she believed to be the root of my triggers. I kept jumping and flinching at the noise of the crash in my mind, my whole body once more tense and shaking, while I tried to keep control of my involuntary movements. I was pressing myself into my chair with every muscle. Magic Lady's belief was that, because I couldn't react or run away when I was in my car, my body had stored and locked up a lot of the trauma instead – I would freeze when triggered and my symptoms would come out physically in shaking. She needed to be able to unbottle that body stress, which was proving tricky. She tried standing us up, pacing, making me move my body to release what I had absorbed. By the time we'd finished our hour, I felt things were still unfinished in my mind. She asked me to score the intensity of the memory – it was still high. Then she said she wanted me to notice how I was triggered throughout the week, but she believed there would still be some processing to do.

The following session was an interesting one, albeit rather frustrating. We didn't conduct EMDR but had a long discussion instead. After telling her about the events of the week – which hadn't shown any improvement in my reactions – I informed her I was now being awoken again in the middle of the night to the bang of the crash, along with experiencing a surge of adrenaline that had my heart racing. I hadn't had these nocturnal flashbacks for a period of time, and I believed they were due to working on that specific point the previous week without any resolutions.

After our discussion, I came to realise I was in fact my own worst enemy. Apparently I had developed the skill of dissociating from my emotions and shutting them down. This was helpful for work in an ordinary setting but no good when trying to recall those emotions to process through trauma. I converted them into somatic symptoms instead – shaking, palpitations etc. I would experience the emotions during flashbacks when triggered at work, but my mind would block them, as a defence mechanism, when I tried to actively recall them during an EMDR session. This is why we had seemingly made no progress the previous week: my mind had felt this part of the memory was too difficult to process emotionally, so it had shut down instead. Magic Lady said she would come up with a different approach for the next session. I was left trying to wrack my own brains as to how to kick my emotional side into gear. I'd gone so long trying to control how I felt, I didn't realise I was inadvertently doing myself damage. I half considered re-exposing myself to the A34 on another visit. If it came to it, I would – anything to keep up my progress.

Three days later, I accidentally resolved the issue on my own.

I was on my way to work for a night shift. I drove down the slip road exiting the A34 towards a major roundabout that merged the road with the motorway – and ahead of me, on the opposite carriageway, was an overturned articulated lorry.

Immediately, panic welled up inside me. I could see the lorry was already being attended to; all three emergency services were there, blue lights flashing everywhere. The road was in the process of being closed. And yet, despite being able to see that help had arrived, despite knowing I was on the other side of the barrier and unable to do anything, I was absolutely distraught. That massive lorry lying on its side was a very real visual to me. It was huge. I couldn't see any other vehicles involved but I could easily visualise up close how much damage a lorry like that would inflict on a whole stationary queue of cars.

I had to wait at those roundabout traffic lights for what seemed like forever; I caught their red glare out of the corner of my eye for the longest time, while my gaze was fixed on the artic, laid out on the road with its belly in the air. I knew I should probably stop the car and pull myself together; that I needed a minute or two. My brain felt it was on the brink of collapsing inwards with flashbacks and I needed to be somewhere safe. But where? There was nowhere to go; nowhere to stop; I was in a live lane of traffic at a busy roundabout. So when the lights changed, I forced everything down and travelled the one junction left on my journey to work. It was a long stretch, about eleven miles, but I knew I had to hang on and keep everything numbed and shoved to the back of my mind. I needed to concentrate on the road; to stay safe and to keep others safe around me.

Finally – *finally* – I made it off the motorway and down the road into work. I parked up and almost ran into the building, up the stairs and onto the balcony. In my safe place, away from prying eyes, out in the fresh air, I then allowed my body to give in to what my brain was screaming. That articulated LGV had absolutely destroyed me. I cried to the point of hyperventilating, totally consumed in emotion and severely triggered. My colleague, Hannah, had seen me arrive and she followed me out. I was aware she was there but I couldn't do anything; couldn't speak, couldn't look at her. I wouldn't allow her to touch me. My whole body trembled violently and I felt as though I'd gone into shock. It was as if it had happened again; as if I'd witnessed the A34 crash all over again. Only this time, I felt I had spent ten minutes analysing it –

exposed to it – by sitting at those traffic lights and not being able to move. The two experiences were almost meshing into one, and I realised that the vicious reaction I was having now was actually how I should have reacted all those years ago. But I'd suppressed everything and not allowed myself to feel. This was how I should have been in 2016: broken.

I was on the balcony for easily an hour, if not longer. Lily had joined us; Hannah had gone into Control to get an update on the lorry driver, who, fortunately, had self-extricated and was ok. They both sat with me, talking to me as I slowly came to. Lily vanished when it was time for the shift to start but Hannah remained with me until I was safe to join too. I felt unbelievably washed out, drained and fluey. It was shocking to me that I'd been triggered so hard for a crash that had already taken place; that I'd just happened to stumble upon. Why was it always me who found the collisions?

With my head now slightly clearer, I knew this wasn't about the overturned artic at all; it was about the previous A34 crash. I also knew something had shifted; released. I had unlocked something in my mind – made contact with the emotions Magic Lady had told me I'd been dissociating from for so long. I talked with Hannah, trying to explain to her that my reaction wasn't just catastrophising or losing control of a severe anxiety – it was actually happening for me. The vehicles had actually crashed before and, in my mind, they repeatedly crashed again when I was triggered. In my addled state, I wasn't sure I was making much sense, but I needed her to understand the severity of it; that I wasn't reacting because of what *could* be, but because of what *had been*, and therefore what *was* each time after that.

I struggled for several days after this incident. I felt incredibly low and tearful, and I could feel myself isolating, pulling away from society. I had plans to meet up with three friends on my days off; I ended up cancelling on two of them and I couldn't wait to leave the third as soon as I'd met with her. I couldn't look her in the eyes and I craved my own company. The time spent on the balcony had pushed me into the pits of despair. I knew I wanted to throw myself into work and keep busy – my old coping mechanism. But working led to triggers and I found that, every time I was triggered, I felt I was a burden on everyone; that Blue Watch must be sick of me. They'd had nearly a year of my drama, yet I clearly wasn't a lot further forward.

Hannah and Lily had been thrust into a helpless situation, watching me have a meltdown, not really knowing what to do or say for the best. I was grateful for their support, their company, and that's all I needed from them, but I hated scaring them. I didn't feel suicidal as such, but that I was a drain on everyone I was leaning on. I figured a lot of people would be better off without having to worry and stress about me, and I hated being that demanding person; hated being in the spotlight the whole time. I knew seeing that lorry had messed my head about, which was why I felt I was such an encumbrance all of a sudden – but it was a sharp slap in the face that was difficult to deal with.

CHAPTER 18
GRIEF

My next EMDR session was a difficult one, but productive. Magic Lady was very interested to hear about my reaction to the rolled-over LGV and seemed to agree with me that something had shifted in my mind. When we started again to work on the memory of the impact of the crash, this time, I found my emotions were fully incorporated, and I cried as we worked. I was still bracing myself, still shaking violently, but she asked me to put crash barriers up in my mind to protect myself and keep me safe when I was recalling the crash.

By the time we'd finished, once again I was wiped out and exhausted. However, I now had a different perspective on the image: it appeared less vivid and I was seeing it from a different angle. It felt almost as if I'd zoomed out on the memory: everything was less focused and intense. We had a bit of a debrief too –

Magic Lady told me the work we had done that night would have opened up a lot of emotions I'd never allowed myself to process before, including grief. It seemed strange to me that I would be grieving for a family I'd never even met. Nevertheless, she warned me I would probably be tearful and very up and down emotionally for the next two to three weeks.

She had some holiday time coming up so explained there would be a longer break before our next session. However, she was aware the anniversary of the crash was approaching on 10th August and, in my emotional state, it would be a difficult thing for me to navigate. She suggested doing something to mark the occasion; having a memorial of sorts. I decided I wanted to lay flowers at the site of the crash and she encouraged this.

The next few days were incredibly tough. I felt wounded, bereft; almost as if I'd just lost someone close to me, rather than that I was trying to deal with the deaths of people I didn't know, which had occurred six years ago. When I slept, I slept deeply, yet still felt exhausted and wrung out.

Two days after that EMDR session, I was back at work. I knew they were short-staffed but were hoping to manage with me still as a supernumerary member. However, it was evident once I got into Control that there was no chance of that, and a plea for overtime was sent out straight away. I was an absolute mess, unable to stop crying. I knew this was showing progress; I knew the outpouring of grief was normal and expected after my last therapy session – but I felt distraught and totally raw. I normally tried to shun my feelings, so this continuous sadness was difficult for me to know what to do with. I felt I was inflicting misery on everyone I spoke to, which didn't help with my already established thoughts of being a burden to others.

I had another meeting with Marcus and I informed Debbie of the situation too, so at least my managers knew what to expect over the next few weeks. I also chatted privately to Clara and Richard, and to Daniel and Jon, who were all as supportive as ever. I did, however, notice something new: normal, run-of-the-mill RTCs no longer invoked a reaction from me. I was still jittery when they were called in, but smaller collisions caused me minimal shaking; barely any symptoms at all. I continued to be triggered by larger incidents, motorway jobs and LGVs, but nevertheless, this was progress.

The following week brought a major heatwave to the UK. Continuous temperatures of over 30°C for more than a week brought devastation in the form of fire. Control was in a condition known as spate, meaning the weather was having significant implications. The phone didn't stop ringing and constant calls often overflowed into neighbouring brigades due to the volume being received. Resources were stretched beyond belief and incident attendances were restricted to life-risk situations only. It seemed as though all three counties were on fire. This started on our day shifts and I found it highly stressful. The constant ringing of the phones seemed to drill into my brain; the pressure of dealing with a permanently manic situation and trying to juggle priorities burnt my tolerance out quickly.

After about three hours of this, I was done. My

senses were overwhelmed, my stress levels were through the roof and, despite not having any RTCs to manage, my body felt triggered as though I was dealing with one. I eventually excused myself from the room, having reached a point where I was tearful and shaky at my desk and my nerves were shredded. Yet again, I found myself sitting on the balcony, feeling guilty for not being able to pull my weight along with the rest of the watch, but also aware that I was still supernumerary and therefore allowed to escape whenever I needed to. I calmed myself – it took a good while to come down completely – then returned to the control room to try again once I felt safe enough. This state of play continued for the rest of the tour into night shifts.

The anniversary on 10th August came round too fast. I tried to keep myself busy and distracted from the heavy grief I was still feeling, catching up with friends on each day off to avoid sitting at home under a dark cloud. The 10th was my second night shift of the tour in the middle of spate. It was exhausting trying to plan anything between shifts but ideal that I would be travelling that route anyway. Richard very kindly offered to drive and accompany me on my trip back to the crash site. I was inordinately grateful that I didn't have to face this on my own. The plan was to meet him at work a couple of hours before my shift was to start. He would drive us there, the journey timed so we'd arrive at the same time as the collision had occurred, at 17:10hrs. Complications arose when I discovered through social media that the A34 was closed for several junctions from mid-morning – including where I was aiming to visit – and this would likely continue for most of the day. I messaged Clara, who I knew was on duty. She told me what the situation was and promised to keep me updated. I, of course, couldn't sleep at all after that. I waited a couple of hours, then, on tenterhooks, figured I would head into work anyway. I needed to get to my shift at some point regardless and couldn't afford to be late as the weather conditions were making it so busy.

I decided to beat the traffic and left home in the early afternoon. At least being in Control meant I would get the updates on the road re-opening. Thankfully, it did, about an hour before I was due to meet Richard. I'd nipped into a shop on the way and purchased flowers; not cut ones, but a plant in a pot that I planned to dig into the soil next to the layby of the A34 junction. As we were in the midst of a heatwave, I knew it was likely the flowers wouldn't survive on the side of a dual carriageway, but it was important to me to plant something living into the ground in memory, rather than leaving stems that would probably end up strewn everywhere.

We headed off together, me feeling anxious about the task ahead and Richard talking the whole way, a distraction I was grateful for. By the time we were climbing the hill on the northbound carriageway, I'd fallen silent but was trying to keep my thoughts stable so I could direct Richard as to where to go. Being driven to the crash site gave me a different perspective, one I'd only experienced once before with Daniel back in March. This time, instead of parking at the junction at the bottom of the hill, we pulled in at the layby near the top. This gave me almost the same view of the carriageway as I'd had that day. We got out of the car and I stared along the road, absorbing the horror once more. My reaction – to my relief – was on a lesser scale than it had been those few months previously; I cried and shook but I wasn't overcome with the flashbacks I'd experienced the first time round. Instead, I was filled with overwhelming grief and sorrow, which I attributed to the EMDR work I had recently done. I dug a small hole in the ground with the trowel I'd brought along with me and planted the flowers in the verge. Standing back to take in the enormity of what they symbolised, and feeling the power of each vehicle thundering by behind me, caused me to dissolve into tears. Richard gave me a hug in support; I could feel myself physically flinching against him each time a lorry passed behind us. The presence of every vehicle instilled a huge fear in me. Despite this, I wanted to walk the length of the layby; I wanted to reach the end and look over at the carriageway. I needed to almost lay the family to rest in my mind. Richard obliged and followed me; allowed me time for my thoughts to go where they needed. After several minutes had passed, we headed back to the car.

By the time we were there, my legs had turned to jelly, my body still shook and I felt totally worn out. I didn't really talk for most of the journey back but I was glad to have company and not to have to drive myself. Richard commented that the change in me was instant and very obvious; he seemed concerned that I appeared to be in a state of shock. When he dropped me off at work, I headed to the restroom to try to gather my thoughts. Sam poked her head in and asked how I was. I'd already warned my watch of my planned trip and they knew the anniversary date. Everybody was very considerate and tried to leave me be.

Work was incredibly difficult that whole night shift. I was dazed and somewhat out of it. I'd had no sleep and it was still as busy as ever with the heat. I was put in an admin position and was thankful to be dealing with less pressured tasks from the back of the room. My head wasn't in the game for the majority of the shift and I was more appreciative than ever of my supernumerary status and my colleagues' understanding.

I slept for most of the next day, recovering from my mental and emotional exhaustion. By the following day, I'd regained myself a little. I still felt shattered but I was also somehow lighter too. The visit had done some good; had allowed me to process my grief further, though I was still wobbly emotionally and as hypervigilant as ever.

A couple of days later, I attended a christening. The church service was overwhelming for me. The full room and the hymns echoing loudly sent my brain into a spin and, despite the happy occasion, I shed a few tears and trembled throughout. I sat with Lucy; she found the day emotional for her own reasons and we ended up supporting each other through it. The celebration afterwards was held in a courtyard space, where I spent most of the afternoon, able to avoid the crowd. Then, the following day, I returned to work – and to my amazement, the commute went smoothly. No tears at all as I travelled by the crash site and, although I couldn't spot the flowers in the split second when I passed, I knew they were there. I had a catch-up with Sam, who had been concerned that my A34 trip may have had a detrimental effect on my wellbeing after seeing me the previous afternoon. I confirmed the opposite to her: that actually I felt as though something had lifted.

My session with Magic Lady that week was an interesting one. I explained to her that I could now take run-of-the-mill RTCs with no problems but that I still struggled with jobs involving major roads, multiple vehicles and LGVs. She believed I had been retraumatised over and over on the back of the crash by then being in the control room every day, and that my subconscious was convinced another call could be as bad as the A34 collision. She described my situation as a kind of complicated secondary trauma: a diagnosis of Complex PTSD as opposed to Single Incident PTSD. We came up with a plan for the following week to conduct EMDR while I wore my headset, as she was keen to address my trauma response when going through taking a call. I also described how overwhelmed I still became day to day, giving examples of working within spate conditions and attending the christening. She said I was still incredibly hypervigilant, my body constantly on edge and braced for something to happen. I was now to practise breathing exercises and find a mindfulness hobby to bring me down to a better level. She labelled me as being very tense but explained that I didn't notice a lot of the anxiety or stress as I was so used to absorbing it. I only noticed when it spilled over my tolerance level: then I couldn't cope. She wanted me to try to be more aware of my body telling me when I was becoming overwhelmed.

This was almost immediately put to the test: I had a ticket to attend a local music festival with the rest of my watch a few days later. I didn't particularly want to go; it had been booked months in advance and I'd thought then that, by this point, I would be in a better place. Nevertheless, I'd paid a fair amount for my ticket and I didn't want PTSD to deter me from living my life. Work colleagues were also keen for me to attend for at least part of the day.

I decided to drive there and not drink, giving myself a quick way to escape if it got too much. When I arrived with my friends and walked onto the field, I immediately felt overwhelmed. The music, the crowds, the busy environment sent my senses spinning. Some of our group had got there ahead of us and set up an area quite close to the stage – great for everyone else but extraordinarily difficult for me to manage. After tolerating a few songs, I excused myself to find somewhere quieter where I could regroup and calm my shaking hands and racing heart. I discovered hammocks set up to the rear of the field and gladly settled myself into one. And that was how my day panned out, alternating between the loud stage, then retreating back to my hammock to calm down. I called it a day at about 18:00hrs and left early. I wasn't sure I was glad I'd attended – I'd enjoyed seeing my colleagues in a social setting but I was a nervous wreck by the end of it and had missed a lot of the performances. My work friends had recently taken to describing my appearance as "eye-y" when I was overwhelmed, as my eyes apparently became very wide, as if I was in shock, when I was triggered. I felt I'd spent the whole time at this festival looking very eye-y. I'd taken all I could bear and I didn't want to encumber my group any more than I'd already done.

The festival actually left me quite ill for the next two days: extremely hypervigilant and in flight mode. I was shaky and anxious, and just wanted to curl up at home and avoid a world that suddenly seemed full of danger. Unfortunately, I couldn't do that, having already made plans with Beth and Georgia. Beth, true to her word after our conversations when I was off sick, had kept in touch; she was feeling better herself and we'd continued to meet frequently. I hadn't seen Georgia much at all, though. She seemed to have dropped off the radar completely and the communication on our group chat was very sporadic. In fact, since my birthday in February I'd only seen her once. That meeting was awkward – I'd made it clear how upset I felt at her vanishing from my life when I needed my friends the most. She'd apologised but hadn't really had a good reason as to why she hadn't kept in contact. My opinion was that she didn't know how to approach or talk to me when I was clearly unwell; she was totally out of her comfort zone. To me, that was no excuse, though: I wasn't asking her to fix me, just to check in every now and again. Now – nearly two months later – they had both finally arranged to meet for coffee the morning after the festival. Admittedly, I'd had no energy to engage in that conversation to organise things. I wasn't in a good place for small talk after recent events. Nevertheless, I tried to make the effort and took myself down to the coffee shop to meet them.

I was a mess: anxious, shaking, on high alert to my surroundings and overly sensitive to the noises around me. I also discovered, when they both arrived, that I couldn't look either of them in the eye. It was all I could do to remain in my seat and push down the instinct, screaming inside me, to run and hide. I knew this was the PTSD hangover after spending the day at a loud music concert and tried to reason with myself to stay calm. But I couldn't engage in their conversation and my stomach was churning, so I didn't partake in drinking coffee either. I sat there while they talked; Beth tried to include me in their chat and did her best to keep things moving. I had nothing to contribute; I was fighting for control of my senses. Georgia looked very uncomfortable and didn't really converse with me – from my silence on our group messages, I think she'd assumed I wasn't going to show. She didn't know how to react to me when I did turn up and it was clear I was having a hard time.

After forty minutes, I'd had enough. I couldn't tolerate the environment around me any longer; I couldn't participate in being sociable; I wanted to do nothing except go home and reset. I made my excuses and left. Beth very kindly messaged me afterwards to check in. I didn't hear from Georgia.

EMDR the next Monday was frustrating. I'd brought my headset along for the session and we worked through recalling recent incidents that had triggered me, trying to recreate the circumstances I'd reacted to and address them. We didn't seem to make much progress so it was back to trying to come up with a different approach. I'd been thinking more about what I could take on as a hobby to help myself, and both Clara and Sasha had suggested wild swimming. Sasha had a friend who did open-water swimming and she asked her for advice and put me in contact with her. The lady who rang me the next day was very friendly, giving up her time to talk to me despite being on holiday at the time. She explained what wild swimming was all about, how it was proven to be so good for both physical and mental health, which group she had joined and where they swam. It was run via a social media page with a county-wide area and lots of different swimming locations. People would post a planned swim and anyone was welcome to join. I loved her enthusiasm and excitement for her pastime, and decided to give it a try, figuring it also matched up with what I'd learned at Harcombe House and with the Surfwell instructors. I ordered beach shoes and a tow float online and planned to join a swim the very next day.

Swimming in the river was a magical experience. The weather was still blazing hot from the heatwave we were enduring, so the water was refreshingly cool. I parked at the starting point and met up with the group of people gathering there, all clutching tow floats – a clear sign who they were! – and together we walked the length of several fields upstream along the river bank. We came to an area known as best access to the water, then swam back down to our starting point. It was peaceful, calming, yet invigorating. I marvelled at the wildlife, and the way the sun, which was low in the sky, made the water sparkle, and I pushed myself to keep up with the group. I'm not the strongest swimmer, nor the fastest, but I'm steady and can keep going for a long time, so I aimed to pace myself to remain in the middle of everyone. I absolutely loved it. I knew in that moment this was something I wanted to continue and I was eager to try out the other swim locations. Being August, it was warm (especially this year), but these swimmers continued all year around.

Cold water swimming is when the water temperature is 14°C or lower, and its benefits include allowing the swimmer to reduce their fight-or-flight response and bring their stress levels down to a manageable level. As the months moved on, I would be able to better control my breathing to deal with the colder temperatures and regulate my state of mind. My first swim burnt off adrenaline in a similar, enjoyable way to my taste of surfing and gave me the bug to do more. Over the next week, I explored more places to go, including swimming alongside a castle, next to some ancient ruins, and in a calm lake, which would be ideal in inclement weather as it took strong currents out of the equation. I met new and interesting people each time I attended and everybody was incredibly welcoming. I was fortunate to have joined a very sociable group.

CHAPTER 19
SETBACK

In September, I had my next EMDR session booked; and it was a tricky one. Magic Lady approved of my outdoor swimming and coincidentally was a wild swimmer herself – which was all I needed to hear to know it was a good choice. I seemed to have stumped her a little with my continual reactions at work and she deemed me complicated with the mesh of my job and my original trauma. The trigger reactions to RTCs that I experienced – few flashbacks these days since working on that last memory but a lot more tears – were described by her as an intense fear, a phobia reaction that would take time to reduce. She wanted me to practise calming myself after every call, even the mundane ones, to try to bring down the accumulating levels of residual anxiety, which should then help when the bigger, scarier jobs came in. She also decided she would try to focus the next EMDR session on the original crash memory again – the point of impact. Once she was happy it had cleared, she suggested working on exposure therapy. I was to ask Keith about obtaining permissions to work on historical call recordings of RTCs. She thought it likely we would need a further six to ten sessions of EMDR following my initial twelve, and said she would write a letter the next week requesting those. I was glad there was a plan of action in place and hoped there would be no complications with further funding being approved.

I spoke with Keith the next time we crossed paths at work. He thought I'd made notable progress and was pleased with how far I'd come. He agreed tentatively to the call recordings and the further EMDR sessions, supporting both requests himself but needing to seek permissions from above him to authorise them. I also had a talk with him about what had started to play on my mind – raising awareness about trauma and PTSD within Control. It was only Keith who had recognised my symptoms; even I had no clue how ill I was. So providing some kind of training for con-ops, and indeed across the fire service, would be beneficial. I wasn't sure yet how to go about this. I knew I would one day like to tell my story, but at that moment in time, I wasn't strong enough to be presenting to various watches on the symptoms I had experienced. I didn't want to come across as preaching either, just because of my personal experience. Keith agreed, though, that more awareness could only be a good thing.

A few cumulative events resulted in me booking sick again the following tour. First, I had a journey from hell driving into work. The A34 developed a sinkhole, which snarled up the flow of vehicles for a number of junctions. I wasn't good with stop-start traffic and the driver directly behind me was tailgating while on her mobile phone. I was on tenterhooks for about an hour, waiting for the moment she would drive into me. The last leg of my now two-and-a-half-hour commute (thanks to the traffic) saw me coming across the tail end of an RTC on the motorway, passing by the wreckage being recovered onto trucks. This was the final straw and I got to work as an overwhelmed, trembling wreck, distressed and crying, and ending up vomiting in the toilets. Lily and Harriet wanted to send me home sick right away but I dug my heels in and refused to go: surely the whole point of being supernumerary meant I didn't have to be counted? They humoured me and planned breaks around me, basically discounting my participation for the night. I was grateful and tried to pull my weight but wasn't well for a lot of the shift. Managing little sleep once I got home and seemingly unable to give my nerves a chance to recover, I was also shaky the following night, although my head was more in the game again by that point.

The next week I came in on my first day shift to be faced with three jobs, one after the other: two separate motorway incidents and then a crash on the A34 involving six cars and a lorry. These sent my brain screaming. I tried to remain in my seat and regain composure; tried to calm myself down amidst it all. Sam was in the room with us for that shift and wasn't used to seeing my reactions. She rather forcefully told me to leave the room as she didn't think sitting there was helping me. I felt like a scolded child and fled to the balcony.

My next EMDR session was that evening – but to get there meant I had to drive past that multi-vehicle RTC on the A34. Seeing the lorry embedded into the central reservation with the van smashed in front was quite a visual for me. Magic Lady set to work and we went over the original memory of the point of collision again, but from a different perspective of focusing on the car containing the family who had passed away that was forced under the lorry. I cried; I felt something shift and we seemed to have made further progress. Then I headed home. Despite being exhausted, I didn't sleep well; vivid dreams punctured my rest.

The following day I was again a mess. I managed most of my shift, until a final lorry RTC came in within the last hour. I tried to manage being triggered – it did feel different this time after my EMDR the previous night, but I was so broken by now that I wasn't coping with anything very well. Lily could see I was struggling and asked me to deal with an unrelated standby instead. I couldn't. I couldn't speak; couldn't pick up the phone. So instead she asked me to go and tidy up the kitchen – a daily routine we all took turns with. It wasn't my job this time but she needed all bums on seats so, sensibly, found a way to remove me and keep the functioning members of the watch on task with what was required. I knew I couldn't help at all at this point and left for the kitchen, where I had a complete meltdown. With the most unfortunate timing, a couple of headquarters staff walked in and tried to get me to talk to them. I refused and told them Control knew where I was and that I didn't need help.

They obviously didn't buy that and headed straight to the control room to report that I was sobbing in the kitchen. Lily and Harriet came to find me, moved me to a side office, finished handover, then returned to me with Clara. They all very kindly stayed with me for about thirty minutes and tried to convince me I should probably book sick if I was struggling this much. Then they handed me over to Anna, the oncoming watch manager, and finally went home.

I talked things over with Anna. I was reluctant to book sick as I only had two more nights to work before I was on leave and would get a break to recover anyway – but in the end I was convinced that it was probably the right thing to do. I realised I was booking sick for the sake of my watch as much as for my own wellbeing. I felt I was such a massive burden. They were short-staffed and stretched, and probably sick of dealing with my drama, which had been ongoing for a year and was seemingly still as intense as ever. I was emotional from being triggered but also gutted that I was causing so many problems for everyone. I'd really struggled with the week I'd had and suddenly felt the watch needed a break from me as much as I needed to just rest. So, Anna booked me sick. I had another tea to help calm my shaking before setting off home. Later, I messaged the three friends who had helped me that afternoon, informing them that, eventually, I had taken their advice.

I slept for most of the weekend, giving my brain and my stress levels a chance to recover. I was learning that it was very easy for things to build up and overcome me: I was in a similar state now as when I'd attended the music festival, and clearly needed to grow more aware of when my body was becoming overwhelmed.

I joined in with a full-moon nighttime swim in the lake, which was very peaceful and settled me further, and at the end of the weekend I felt more myself again. So I booked fit and set about making plans for my time off. This included a trip to the spa for Debbie's birthday – an experience that was mostly enjoyable, although the silent chamber with hot stone benches was *deathly* silent and caused my thoughts to intrude, making me shake once more. I excused myself from that room and went to calm myself in the garden instead. I also had yet another Occupational Health appointment to contend with, as I seemed to automatically trigger a phone call with them when booking sick with PTSD. They were very good and acknowledged that this was just a setback, which wasn't unusual during periods of rehabilitation. They also noted that it was vital for my recovery to remain in the workplace where possible. I was relieved by this – they actively encouraged me to book fit and not to go sick as soon as I started to struggle. I appreciated their understanding, and the support in maintaining my supernumerary status for as long as was necessary.

I returned to work after my sickness and my leave to good and bad news. The good news was that I was also returning to instructing JCs – and that EMDR had made significant progress there. Whereas before the summer holidays I was reacting rather severely to the station turnouts, now they had little effect on me. I was incredibly aware of when they sounded and what that meant but, other than my heart leaping, and feeling a bit jittery, my body didn't react. Finally, real progress could be seen and I was so relieved. I could now instruct with no fear of having to leave the room and I was no longer breaking down in front of my colleagues.

The bad news was back in Control. On my first shift back, I was asked into Keith's office. He gently broke it to me that the watch had reported concerns. They were now becoming distressed themselves when I found myself triggered: getting upset seeing me struggle and feeling anxious when calls came in that they knew would affect me. This hit me like a punch to the stomach. When triggered, I was totally absorbed within myself and my own senses. I wasn't aware of anyone around me, let alone the effect my response was having on them. I was devastated and felt even more like such a burden. I thought I had a safe space; it had never ever crossed my mind that I was actually upsetting others. I hated that I was doing that to them.

Keith's suggestion was to set up a terminal in the training room next door. If I reacted, I could leave to alleviate my colleagues' stress but still see what was happening from the next room if I needed to follow the incident in its entirety. This seemed to be a good middle ground to appease everyone.

I spoke to all my colleagues individually after my meeting with Keith; I wanted to apologise for making them feel upset, but also to thank them for voicing their concerns and being sensitive about it. The last thing I wanted was for them to pick up any secondary trauma through my experiences, so I was grateful they were able to come forward when they started to struggle. Nevertheless, I was quite down when I returned home that evening. I shed a few tears and didn't sleep well, feeling that my despair was seemingly seeping into others.

CHAPTER 20
PROGRESS

The following day saw my luck continue in similar fashion. It was a chilly Sunday morning, 25th September 2022. I headed off to my second day shift and joined the motorway, which was fairly clear with it being early. As I headed down the junction, I noticed two articulated lorries in front of me, one pulling into the second lane, the other remaining in the first. Both had switched their hazards on and were braking hard. I manoeuvred my car into the third lane and, peeking round them, realised a car had rolled over in the middle of the carriageway. It was upside down, straddling lanes one and two, with debris covering the third, and it was smoking where it had clearly just come to a stop. I also hit my brakes, and plonked my car neatly next to the lorry in the middle lane, trying to block off the last part of the carriageway as best I could with my little hatchback. I grabbed my phone, dialled 999 with trembling hands and requested fire. As the operator transferred me, I got out of my car and moved towards the wreckage.

I was put through to a colleague, Toni, although I didn't recognise her voice until towards the end of the call. I stated who I was – work would need to know my situation and also that I would be late for shift – and I gave my location exactly as I knew it would have to be entered on our computer system. I described the situation in front of me: one overturned car; two male adults trapped inside. One appeared to have a broken leg and the other a nasty head injury. It wasn't until the end of the call, when Toni asked me if I was ok, that my brain kicked into gear a little more and I realised who she was. I was on a recorded line so didn't want to be discussing my own wellbeing. I also wanted to hang up as quickly as possible to help the casualties in front of me. So I avoided her question and instead told her I needed to go and assist. I cut the call.

I realised at that moment that tears were streaming down my face. I wiped them away, took a deep breath to steady myself and moved closer to speak to the two men.

They were both conscious. The male with the broken femur (I'll call him Omar) seemed trapped but was talking to me quite level-headedly. The second casualty – Ali – was bleeding from a nasty head wound and seemed insistent on crawling out of the upside-down vehicle, dragging himself over the broken glass shards sprinkled everywhere. Traffic by now was squeezing past my car and whooshing away. I walked towards the next car in line, put my hands up to signal them to stop and the rest came to a halt too. Another helper, who had since joined me, darted off towards the temporarily stationary traffic to make sure they held their static position, as I turned back to the injured men.

Ali pulled himself free before I could get to him, but once out – still on the ground – he seemed confused and agitated. He said he had pain in his back and neck. I kept him still on the ground, bracing his neck as well as I could to keep him immobile and try to prevent further injury. Positioning myself between Ali and the car, I was able to talk to both him and Omar and keep them alert. Omar had pulled out his mobile and was calling family members to tell them what had happened. He then dialled a number so that Ali could speak to his mum. I ended up taking the phone from him as his distress became increasingly palpable; the call was lengthening and I could hear his mother panicking on the other end as Ali's anguish magnified. After assuring his mum that both men had people helping them and that the emergency services were on their way, I hung up and gave the phone back to Omar.

A driver threw me his coat, which I laid over Ali who was now feeling cold – likely a mixture of shock and having to lie on the ground. His head wound seemed to have stopped actively bleeding, so I didn't touch it. I continued to keep the two men talking: found out where they'd come from and where they were headed. They had apparently left early on their drive and one of them had fallen asleep at the wheel. The car had hit the barrier and rolled.

Before long, the first fire crew arrived; some were my old colleagues from my on-call days, and I gave them a brief handover explaining the situation. They threw me a pair of blood gloves and let me carry on with Ali, while they moved round to the other side of the car to help with extricating Omar. Soon, both police and ambulance joined us. The police seemed overly keen to clear the road and reopen it to traffic. I passed them my keys so they could move my car once they got the say-so. However, the paramedics and firefighters were refusing to allow traffic to flow with Ali still on the ground so close to the third lane. I remained in situ, supporting his head and neck while the medical crew worked. Eventually, he was boarded and taken to the ambulance for transportation. Omar was in a worse state but was still conscious by the time he too was taken away to hospital. A police officer pulled me aside to find me some wipes – looking down, I realised I was covered in blood. I was allowed to be part of the hot debrief, a talk between services on the events of an incident, and I also chatted to the fire officer, who had arrived in his car, after he recognised me as Control staff.

Once everybody began to pack up, I slipped away. My car had been relocated onto the hard shoulder in front of the blue light vehicles. Checking my phone before I drove away, I found missed calls from Control, Toni, and a message from Toni too. I'd clearly worried a lot of people. I got off the hard shoulder and proceeded to the next junction before calling them back. That would take me to the A34 where I could find a layby to stop in and ring them safely. On my way, I marvelled at how my body was behaving. I felt almost energised, triumphant: I had not only come across an RTC but had actively participated in the events following it. I was relieved that something in my brain had kicked in and allowed me to react instinctively, like a muscle memory. I was incredibly shaky and could sense the force of adrenaline flooding through my bloodstream – but I felt good and, despite the men's injuries, I seemed to be on a bit of a high. It was different to the other times. I'd been able to help – do something – and I knew the outcome for both casualties was likely to be ok. It was one hell of a difference from witnessing fatalities and being unable to do anything about them.

I stopped the car when I was next able to and made a quick call to Control. Sam had specifically requested I speak to her, so I was put through. I assured her I was doing all right; in fact, managing better than I ever thought I would. She seemed to take some comfort from that. I told her when I was due to arrive at Control, then continued with my journey, making a mental note to text Toni once there to thank her for her kindness.

I walked into the control room an hour later, still wearing clothes covered in blood. I'd had to stop at a drive-through en route to buy a hot chocolate, feeling the need for sugar to control my tremors and steady my nerves. My colleagues, it turned out, had been a little frantic, convinced I would end up in the back of an ambulance myself with a full-blown PTSD meltdown. Instead, I'd coped remarkably well. I felt rather chuffed with myself, and buoyed that perhaps progress was being made after all. I excused myself to shower and change into clean clothes, then belatedly started my working day.

My EMDR session just a few days later produced

an interesting discussion. Magic Lady seemed fascinated and pleased that I'd managed to step up and deal with the rolled-over car, and we talked about it in depth. At the risk of sounding a little morbid, the event did seem to have boosted my recovery somewhat. I'd been absolutely terrified and overcome – my violent shaking, tears and the forceful flood of adrenaline had indicated that – yet somehow, I was able to lock that immediate reaction away, as I would with a 999 call, and deal with the emergency situation laid out in front of me, despite it spanning a prolonged period. By the time the response to the crash had been played out, I'd burnt off a lot of that initial fight-or-flight by taking action. The positive outcome meant my brain didn't then spiral – I seemed relieved and pleased instead. I dreaded to think what I would have been reduced to had it not ended well; I imagined a fatality would have sent me spinning out of control. However, I was confident, based on this experience, that I would have been able to maintain composure until my assistance was no longer needed.

Our previous session on the back of my sickness had seen us going over coping strategies, as I was still incredibly tense and hypervigilant day to day; evidently it wasn't taking much for pressures to mount up, leaving me distressed and overwhelmed. I'd been attempting to be aware of this – for example, noticing if I was bracing my muscles or holding my breath in tense anticipation while driving – and Magic Lady had tried to explain that, although I'd witnessed something horrific, that didn't mean my body had to be ready and prepared the rest of the time, as the likelihood of history repeating itself was a slim one. I was to try to focus on overriding this automatic response.

This following session then had a little bit of an I-told-you-so vibe to it: less than a week after that advice, I had yet again witnessed something happen in front of me. I explained that that seemed to be how my luck was cursed – in the space of a few months, I'd come across the rollover on Christmas Eve, the artic lorry that had turned over, and now this most recent crash. My commute these days involved a one-hundred-and-twenty-six-mile round trip, spanning three major roads so, statistically, I *was* going to come across more incidents than the average driver. However, this latest event proved I was driving more safely than ever and was clearly capable of dealing with any incidents that might unravel in front of me.

Time passed and suddenly we were in October. Magic Lady asked me to pick some call recordings at work, and ran through how to listen to them in a safe, controlled environment, as a bit of an exposure-therapy homework task. It was a delicate line to walk between being vulnerable and improving with each recording, and retraumatising myself each time – so it had to be done correctly. Work had approved the use of old calls, with my agreement that they remained within the workplace to adhere to data protection rules. After noting down which incident numbers I wanted to retrieve, a colleague very kindly placed them on a memory stick for me. I'd thought carefully about which calls to relive, and chose a mixture of incidents that I vividly remembered in recent months, scaling up in severity from run-of-the-mill RTCs to the recording of the initial A34 collision. Working on these was incredibly difficult and emotional. I would be triggered, quite often crying and shaking, and my colleagues described me as eye-y after every session. I would limit myself to about an hour of working on them each shift, shutting myself up in another room where I wouldn't be disturbed or startled.

Meanwhile, Magic Lady came up with an alternative approach to assist me. She had consulted with a colleague, explaining the situation and the progress that had been made, but noting I was still being quite severely triggered with specific incidents. The call recordings seemed to take the edge off my anxiety levels a little, and I did become desensitised to most of the historical calls with time, but that didn't seem to convert into a non-reaction with live calls. The colleague had suggested we focus on the night shift directly after the A34 crash, indicating that it sounded as though I'd had a lot of trauma associated with that shift, and had basically undertaken working it within a state of shock. This theory explained, too, why I would often go eye-y, as my watch described it: I would seemingly revert back to a shocked state when I was triggered.

Magic Lady picked my brains about hotspots in my memory of that shift and I talked her through my experience. There seemed to be two things that stuck in my mind: the chat I'd had with the station manager at the time and reviewing the photographs together, and the memories of being within Control, sitting on the primary 9s position and waiting anxiously as each radio message was taken from across the room. This information then formulated our plan of action for our next sessions. Magic Lady also explained a little more about my diagnosis of Complex PTSD. CPTSD is caused by multiple incidents of trauma, and accounted for why I'd been deemed a complicated case throughout my treatment. I'd experienced the initial crash, which was traumatising enough, but had then embarked on a fifteen-hour night shift that had embedded that experience while I was still in shock, and retraumatised me repeatedly. Work incidents had then added to that over and over again, until the trauma memories were all interlinked. I've interpreted it as like having a tangled ball of string in my brain. One memory strand can be pulled at when dealing with an RTC at work, for example, but that then triggers the intertwined mess of trauma that's built up in my mind, leading me to have a massive reaction. It all seemed to make sense but also meant that, after EMDR had helped me process everything it could, I would still be left with residual PTSD symptoms due to the complex way my brain had become rewired – comparable to a brain injury. It was interesting to understand how it all worked but rather scary to think I might always have to fight for control over this.

Frustratingly, there was a delay in approval of the financing for the further sessions that had been agreed with the brigade, meaning my appointments were halted until we had the confirmation to proceed. Magic Lady also caught Covid, so that pushed our next meeting back further. It ended up being a period of almost six weeks before we could pick up where we'd left off.

In the meantime, I managed the best I could, trying to ride out stresses in my personal life: after all this time, my vulnerable mum, my brother and my dad all caught Covid. They were poorly, but fortunately able to recover at home without medical intervention, which is what I'd feared would be needed; Mabel, the rabbit also ruptured a disc in her spine, so I had to ferry her back and forth to the vet for treatment; and my car went in to be repaired after someone pranged it when it was parked up, meaning I then had to drive already scary journeys in a 4x4 courtesy car. These were all normal life events but I seemed to spiral, still having no reserves or capacity to deal with things when they went wrong. I confined myself to my house, trying to calm my shredded nerves. I did attempt a trip to the supermarket but, overwhelmed, left fairly swiftly and empty-handed. I isolated myself after that. Spending four consecutive days off at home, without having to face the world, seemed to reset my brain and I was able to manage better again.

On 1st November, I received a boost to my confidence. After talking to Keith about my progress, and discussing things with Debbie and Marcus, I agreed to come off supernumerary crewing from this date. I was now a fully-fledged, counted member of the crew. It was scary, having been deemed an extra since returning to work all the way back in April, but they seemed to think I had made enough significant progress to once again be productive. I was still clearly in therapy and healing; still sent wobbly by large RTCs; still having emotional off days. But my watch were all aware of the situation, and the fact they felt they could trust me as a con-op again, rather than my being, in my own eyes at least, a burden for them, was huge. I was warned to take it slowly; they also made sure I was feeling confident enough to come off my supernumerary status. But I felt easier with the decision than I had done back in the summer with my first attempt, so I agreed to put myself out there and give it a go. It was, in a way, a massive relief: just a few short months back, I'd been doubting whether I would ever be able to tolerate the job and my working environment again. For my managers to tell me this had now been achieved, and for them to still have faith in me, was an incredible weight lifted.

Around this time, through the Fire Fighters Charity, I saw it advertised that there was to be an Emergency Services Mental Health Symposium held at a venue less than half an hour away from me. It was two days of lectures and talks, personal experiences and education, with organisations being represented from all over the country. It was free to emergency services staff and was taking place in a couple of weeks' time, when, conveniently, I was on my rota days off. I signed up, then forwarded the link around the control room to invite all my colleagues to join me. Alison seemed interested and put her name down to attend.

This symposium had me thinking back to my discussion with Keith about raising awareness of trauma and PTSD in the workplace. When I chatted to Richard about it, explaining about the symposium and that I wanted, somehow, to make a difference, his idea was to write this: a book, so people could read about it and learn from someone with first-hand experience. I was sceptical at first and almost laughed it off as a joke. People wouldn't want to read about me, surely? It wasn't that interesting a story and, as I've mentioned, I didn't want to come off as preaching to others. However, after the idea embedded a bit, I figured that actually it could be good for me to put my thoughts down onto paper. So, I started a scrambled kind of writing – and my words came pouring out.

The symposium was a humbling, emotional, draining experience. It opened with a panel of speakers from all three emergency services, who talked about their personal struggles with their mental health. They spoke frankly, bravely, and I was in awe of their strength and perseverance in overcoming their demons. The venue was set up with two lecture halls running relevant talks simultaneously. They were all available to attend and you could pick and choose what would benefit you most. There was a foyer filled with various organisations to assist with emergency services personnel, including representatives from the Fire Fighters Charity and Surfwell, and many therapy dogs, who were available at all times for cuddles and so that participants could chat with their handlers. There was also a calm room set up – a retreat for anyone to retire to if they became overwhelmed.

Two particular talks stood out to me over the course of the couple of days. The first was from a neighbouring fire service over the border from us. They spoke a lot about dealing with trauma experiences and PTSD; how to care for firefighters who had dealt with harrowing scenes in the course of their job; what was in place to recognise, support and address their trauma. It all sounded very good and well thought out, but I had one burning issue, which I voiced in the Q&A session afterwards: what about Control staff? What strategies had been put in place to recognise their trauma? To support their struggles?

My question was met with silence; then a hesitant answer: they didn't know. They didn't believe anything like this was in place for con-ops.

I thanked them, but it set my mind whirring. Control staff seemingly were not part of this equation. As often is the case, they were being forgotten about. Now, we may not run into burning buildings, but Control staff are the first point of contact with anything traumatic. We deal with all callers and, in the case of my own workplace, that exposure is tripled through working across three counties. It was something I felt was a serious oversight that needed to be addressed. I knew our perspectives were different from the operational crews – someone at the symposium described it accurately: when crews attend a scene, they get to see an incident unfold like a film in front of them, vividly, in 3D. Control room staff experiences are, instead, like reading a book – we're given the rough plot and some details, but the rest of the information is for us to fill in with our imaginations and, often, with missing pages. This eventually will take its toll if steps aren't implemented to intervene.

The second lecture that spoke to me was a personal account – a British Transport Police officer who had come to tell his story of PTSD. He talked about his experiences of attending horrendous train crashes, and showed slides holding images of said incidents. He spoke of his symptoms, his diagnosis; the journey he'd been on to get to where he was now – helping others within the police suffering from trauma, alongside his faithful therapy dog. He got a little emotional while speaking and you could have heard a pin drop in the room. For me, it was as though I was suddenly winded; his whole talk seemed to mirror my own story.

Even the devastation of derailed trains reminded me of the tangled messes of cars I'd seen. It completely blindsided me and I was triggered. By the end of his delivery, I was a sobbing, trembling mess in a state of shock.

As people left for lunch, I remained in my seat and the speaker came to talk to me. I was able to fuss his dog, and I calmed and came to as he spoke, until my brain eventually clicked back into gear. Then we swapped experiences. He told me how much he had benefitted from EMDR and spoke of how he dealt with things today, years later. His manner and the way he described his recovery reminded me very much of my talks with Jon and what he had managed to achieve. We even compared tattoos – he had also got inked to symbolise the journey he'd been on. I was so very grateful for his kindness and his time, and he promised to find me later in the day to check in and continue chatting, which we did. Strangely, I wasn't horrified with myself for breaking down in a room full of hundreds of strangers; I knew everything was still very raw for me and this man's story had struck a chord. And, after all, wasn't that what this event was all about?

I came away from that symposium armed with a lot of information that I hoped to pass on to my brigade.

The following week, I had a long discussion (nearly an hour and a half) with Keith, explaining what I'd learnt and what I hoped to achieve. I'd also jotted some ideas down – a proposal of a kind. He promised to set up a meeting with the wellbeing manager to discuss my points, some of which he felt weren't really achievable while others definitely had merit to progress further. I was happy with that. The meeting couldn't take place for several weeks for various reasons, but I was in no rush. I felt optimistic that out of all the darkness I had endured, something good could come from it.

The night after the symposium, an overtime shift became available in Control. Until that point, I'd avoided overtime. I wasn't long out of being supernumerary and didn't want to overdo it by pushing too hard, too fast. This shift, though, came about towards the end of November and I'd had a few weeks adjusting by then. I rang in to offer my services and spoke to Clara: she told me Daniel was one of those managing the shift. I was bolstered by this as he had been supporting me the whole way through with my PTSD. Clara and Daniel talked to each other and Daniel then messaged me to ask what desk position I'd prefer and what break would work best for me. It was very thoughtful but I was happy to be entirely flexible. My only request was to be able to mirror Daniel's breaks. Then, if I had a wobble, he would be prepared and know how to deal with it. He was happy to accommodate this, as were the rest of the watch when he confirmed it with them.

My long journey to do my overtime had already caused me to shake; battling through Friday night rush hour wasn't enjoyable. Nevertheless, I got there in good time to be able to talk to Red Watch beforehand. I explained, briefly, what had been going on; what I might experience in the control room as a trigger, and how I might react if that happened. I also told them that, if it did, they should ignore me. It could be distressing to see me, but it was a normal, regular occurrence for me now. I assured them I'd be all right – it just took a bit of time to ride it out and get my head back in the game. They accepted this and were incredibly kind.

Most of the shift was uneventful; until towards the end in the morning, when we received reports of a multi-vehicle RTC on the motorway. I worked my job, did what I had to do, but could feel the shutters coming down in my brain and my nerves screaming to flee. Daniel, in a later discussion, told me the effect on me was instant: my whole demeanour changed abruptly. The rest of the watch took it in their stride, ignoring me as I'd asked them to and talking around me. I was able to stay in the game in terms of doing my job, but my triggered state of fear meant I could do no more than that. I couldn't look them in the eye or join in the conversations, focusing instead on trying to calm my racing heart and erratic breathing. When I eventually unclenched, my flight mode subsided and I was able to rejoin the room on a social level little by little. It was a rather vulnerable experience to be triggered in front of new colleagues, who had never experienced me in the midst of a PTSD episode, and I was glad to have Daniel there, keeping an eye. He told me afterwards that I was majorly improved from when he'd seen me in the earlier days – completely shutting down to flashbacks on the back of a fire station turnout. It was encouraging to hear that. I found that listening to other people's perspectives on my reaction was the best way to gauge my progress. I still felt terrified whenever it happened, so my peers' honest opinions were valued, and I came away from that shift with mixed emotions but glad I'd pushed myself to do it.

The first shift back next tour saw me wobbly, emotional, withdrawn and hypervigilant. My sleep had featured nightmares and nocturnal flashbacks, which had previously stopped. I figured it was overwhelm again on the back of the symposium and then my first overtime shift the next night. However, after a very up-and-down time at work, and another sleep, I was a lot more settled the following day.

The next week, the first in December, saw my EMDR sessions start up again. Magic Lady confirmed what I'd suspected: I was totally overwhelmed by events and had probably triggered myself repeatedly at the symposium. She believed I was still boxing a lot of emotions away to be able to deal with day to day. My brain then did most of my processing at night, hence the increase in nightmares and sleep disturbances when I was particularly stressed. It all seemed to make sense. She approved of the symposium and my findings, though, and was supportive of both my continued exposure to call recordings and my beginning to write this book, which often caused me to cry or shake as I typed but gave me a feeling of catharsis when working on it.

She then started our EMDR work on that traumatic night shift, many years ago.

CHAPTER 21
BREAKTHROUGH

Magic Lady positioned herself opposite me and asked me to recall the first part of the memory we were to work on. This was conversing with my then station manager, who had just got back from the A34 crash to discover that I'd witnessed it. I remembered talking to him about it, him offering to show me photos of the devastation, and my morbid curiosity in wanting to see the pictures of the crash in its entirety, rather than just having my split-second perspective from the other side of the carriageway. Magic Lady began to move her fingers, stopping at regular intervals.

Those images seemed to be burned into my soul, although until I was actively recalling them, I had no idea how vivid they still were. They didn't appear to be photos in my perspective, but rather at the forefront of my memory, like an actual scene laid out in front of me. I seemed to be connecting my emotions and the experience of witnessing and hearing that crash with seeing those devastating images. She asked me to let my mind go where it needed to so as to make those pictures less intense. By the end of the session, I had cried, tensed, shaken violently; but now, when recalling the memory, I could see the photos in the background, distant on a computer screen on the station manager's desk while the two of us continued our chat. Those images, although still present and not forgotten, had been processed to a point where they were no longer the focal point of my recall.

I was astounded, relieved, wiped out and still very shaky. However, something, I knew, had shifted; more progress had been made. I said thank you and left, knowing I was in for a rough couple of days of processing but grateful we'd found another route to go down that seemed to be working.

I was booked in again the following week, which turned out to be a hugely stressful session. First, a couple of days beforehand, I was asked to drive my mum to hospital for a minor procedure in the city. This required me to drive her on the A34 in frozen, snowy conditions. My mum was nervous about her surgery and unaware of both my reluctance to have passengers in my vehicle and my feelings about driving that particular road. I hadn't talked to her about it, not wanting to worry her and appear vulnerable. So, I absorbed my stress as best I could and hid my emotions inside so as not to alarm her.

After dropping her off, I had to wait, as it was day surgery and I was her lift home again. I'd discovered there was an issue with my front tyre, which meant that, instead of the leisurely day I'd hoped for to distract myself, I ended up frantically searching for a car workshop with availability to sort my wheel out before she needed collecting. I managed to find one company with a slot free and waited on tenterhooks. Twenty minutes after my car was fixed, I received the call to go and fetch her. She seemed as well as could be expected and the surgery had been successful but, again, I felt she needed me to be strong to support her. I found myself picking my way through what had become rush hour traffic, tensed and braced as if the world was about to end. My mum was sleepy from the anaesthesia and didn't notice that I wasn't in a chatty mood. We made it home and I could finally breathe again.

The next day, I was like a rabbit in headlights at work; the overwhelm from suppressing my stress levels the previous day was massive. I'd calmed down enough by the following shift to be ready for my next EMDR session afterwards, but it ended up being horrendously difficult.

We started to process my memories of actually being in the control room on the night of the crash. I was on Green Watch back then and could recall everything: I was positioned on primary 9s and remembered the unbelievable levels of anxiety, terror, dread and anticipation each time the radio messages came in; waiting to hear updates and frequently checking the log on my screen. Across the room from me was the primary radio position, that seat filled by Richard that night. I knew who else was in the room and where they were sitting. As I recalled the memory, though, everyone else seemed insignificant and faded into the background. I was hyper-focused on the messages Richard was receiving. One in particular described quite vividly the ten-tonne lorry resting on two wheels with the car wedged underneath it. LGV recovery would be needed before the occupants of that vehicle could be extricated.

Magic Lady asked me to focus on that – each time I did so and recalled Richard typing, my brain would shoot me back to being in my own car on the A34 and watching it happen. It was incredibly distressing – and astounding how interwoven those two memories were.

And suddenly, it made sense.

This was why I was having such a hard time dealing with my triggers at work. All the feelings I'd had on that night mirrored my current experiences when receiving 9s calls into Control; that was where the overwhelming anxiety and terror came from. Every time I dealt with an RTC, my brain would ping me straight back to watching that family die. The devastation was repeated again and again.

We continued like this for an hour before calling it a night and reducing my stress levels to a manageable level to drive home. Magic Lady asked me to rate how distressing the memory was at the end of our session. It still seemed high to me and I felt we'd opened something up but left it unfinished. I couldn't wait to leave. I was absolutely wrung out.

The rest of the week wasn't good, although for some reason I didn't relate that to the events of my EMDR session. At handover one shift, White Watch came in and Alison tried to enthusiastically have a chat with me, asking me about my open water swimming. However, I was trembling and nowhere near capable of engaging in conversation, telling her rather more sharply than I intended that I couldn't talk right now. Glancing at her, I could see she was wounded at my response. I hadn't meant to sound so abrupt but ignoring her would have been just as rude, and they were the only two options at my disposal at that point. I blanked a fellow con-op sitting next to me, too, to avoid having to engage in more conversation. The whole room fell momentarily silent at my response to Alison. Ten minutes afterwards, I left, sure that I was the topic of conversation once I'd gone.

I messaged Alison the next day, apologising and explaining that I'd been in an overwhelmed, hypervigilant state and I couldn't even make eye contact with anyone, let alone chat. I hoped, after attending the symposium together, that she would understand a little and not take it personally. She graciously accepted my apology. I also said sorry to the con-op I'd ignored and explained to her too. This ended up being a good conversation as she asked lots of questions, which I was happy to answer. I then worked an extra night shift that tour with Green Watch, some overtime that, in hindsight, wasn't a wise move. This was my second extra shift and I did what I'd done with my first: spoke to the watch and explained I was a bit broken, what might happen and that they should just let me be if I ended up becoming triggered. I, for some reason, hadn't counted on the fact that my mind was still in a scrambled, vulnerable state from exploring a horrific memory in EMDR, then leaving things unfinished. I'd also not banked on the fact that, within just a couple of hours, we would receive a call to a fatal RTC – a head-on collision caused by a drunk driver just one week before

Christmas. I spiralled. I tried to remain focused; in control. However, my head was having none of it and my body flooded with adrenaline, horror and dread. I'm sure if my own watch had been there, they would have described me as very eye-y.

I sat out the job; I took the radio messages as was deemed my responsibility and I tried not to let an overwhelming fear overtake me. In the end, I had to excuse myself and went to vomit in the toilets. It had been a while since I'd been sick through stress. My poor colleagues, unused to my being triggered, looked on helplessly; the watch manager in particular seemed distraught at my reaction. I hated myself for that. I'd wanted to do the overtime appearing competent and improved. I felt as though I'd put them all in an awkward position and scared them unnecessarily. At the end of the shift, I went home feeling extremely low and frustrated with myself, and still in a bad state from the RTC.

Jon happened to check in that day. I spoke to him at length about what had happened. I also had several chats and a very long phone conversation with Richard. I needed to reach out and vent. I was furious with myself, tearful, and for the next couple of days I struggled to cope.

Two days after this was our work Christmas do. I still felt unstable and vulnerable and I wasn't looking forward to the event, which was an afternoon tea and cocktails. However, I also refused to let this thing completely beat me. Instead, I decided to put measures in place to make things a little easier. I drove myself, as I'd done with social events before, and stuck to mocktails, which gave me an escape route at any point.

I also knew Red Watch were on duty at the time and I messaged Daniel to ask if he'd mind my swinging by Control afterwards for a cuppa to decompress, before driving all the way home.

To my relief, the venue, being mid-afternoon, was fairly empty. But with both Blue and Green Watches having a joint do, I still felt rather overwhelmed at the bustle of so many people around me, the voices all echoing loudly in the spacious room. I took the time to speak to and apologise to the watch manager of Greens for my behaviour during the overtime shift; I knew I'd scared him and I tried to reassure him that I was ok and just having a rather vulnerable week.

The afternoon seemed to pass slowly. I'd positioned myself at the end of the table to feel less confined and it was nice to see everyone outside of the working environment. However, by the end of our three-hour slot, I was jittery and ready to leave. Most of our group went on to a local pub, whereas I took the opportunity to bid them goodbye and headed to Control. By the time I reached work, I was shaking quite badly. I walked straight into the control room, saw where Daniel was sitting and made a beeline for him. I wasn't able to say a lot, feeling once again that week that I was in flight mode.

Daniel clocked my appearance immediately and suggested we go to the kitchen to make a tea. The rest of the watch had gone quiet and the two managers in charge that day looked rather concerned, insisting Daniel should leave and take care of me. It was only once we'd reached the kitchen Daniel revealed he'd forgotten to warn the rest of the watch that I would be showing up – which explained their shocked faces! I spent a couple of hours there, talking to several people until I was steady and once again safe to drive. When I got home, I did a tally: in the space of a week, I'd managed to worry or upset every single watch I worked with. Blues, in their usual, patient way, had put up with my wobbly head for the whole tour; I'd insulted Whites, scared Greens and now shocked Reds. I felt more of a burden than ever. And so, so guilty.

My next EMDR session was scheduled for two days later, just a few days before Christmas. Magic Lady was concerned that I'd been in such a distressed state for the duration of the week, and we immediately got to work where we'd left off: I recalled the night shift post-crash, with my focus on Richard as he took the radio messages that came in. I was immediately back in hell. The imagery kept changing; my memories intertwining and mixing everything up. I would watch him type at his computer, then all of a sudden, the lorry was crashing into a queue of stationary cars. But then this started to happen *in Control, between our desks in the centre of the room.* Richard didn't flinch or even look up; my memory of him was that he continued to carry out his job professionally, seemingly oblivious to the LGV killing people in front of us. I, however, was utterly distraught that this was happening again, so realistically, and in the middle of our workspace.

Magic Lady paused me, pulled me back and told me to breathe, as I seemed to have forgotten to do that. Then we started again: several times over, the vehicles collided between our desks, with me horror-struck and Richard blissfully unaware of it all. Then the image started to change; to morph. Instead of the crash happening in the control room, my brain altered the perspective and I was suddenly transported back to the side of the A34, but while still sitting at my desk. I was on the southbound carriageway, as I was on the day; on the northbound side, behind the tangled mess of vehicles, was Richard, also at his desk and still typing up messages, but without seeming to have noticed the change in venue.

Magic Lady paused me again; I breathed, withdrew, then restarted the recollection. After several reruns, the image changed again. This time I was back in the control room, as was Richard. I was hyper-focused on my screen, looking at the incident log as Richard typed. Then, horrified, I found myself at my desk, but strapped into my car seat and clenching so hard, I hurt all over. My seatbelt was digging into my shoulder as I craned forward intensely to watch the screen update. By now, my whole body was screaming: I'd watched and relived the family dying over and over, and the change of scene and perspective each time was exhausting and terrifying.

We withdrew once again and concentrated on my breathing. Time was ticking away but neither of us wanted to end the session – with a prolonged Christmas break afterwards – without this memory being resolved. Magic Lady tried to come up with solutions that would ease my horror and remove me from the distressing situation within my brain. She encouraged me to try to almost zoom out from the memory – take in the images of the other people I knew were there but who were inconsequential. Her intention was to move my rigid focus away from my computer screen: could I look at something else? My emails on the admin PC or why not stare at a different screen? This didn't work; my subconscious wouldn't allow me to draw my gaze away from the disaster unfolding in front of me.

Unexpectedly, my brain offered another solution, in the form of a different but real memory. As Richard had been a support throughout my whole PTSD fight, there had been many instances when we'd both been on the balcony outside in the fresh air, with me breaking away from an intense situation, trying to calm down and collect my thoughts. So, my recollections seeming to mix yet again, when running through the memory of the control room once more, I was able to escape the distress and remove myself from the situation to the balcony with Richard.

Once my brain had found a way out of that loop of destruction, I apparently visibly relaxed in front of Magic Lady. When she asked me to, I could now visualise the others who were in the control room, although they weren't in focus. They were still unflinching, unaffected by the situation – in particular, my previous crew manager, who was stating with some surprise that she didn't realise I was bothered by things like this. My memories were so mixed up and interlinked! That comment, I knew, originated not from this crash but from the Christmas period more than a year later. Yet I seemed to be taking her words as a personal assault. They mirrored my own disappointed views in myself: I didn't *want* to be bothered by things like this. My subconscious seemed to be doing its damnedest to compensate for my "weakness" through PTSD by trying to fight for control – of everything; quashing my emotions and mentally resisting the process of dealing with the memories.

We worked on lessening that intense control in my mind: mentally chaining myself to my desk wouldn't make me stronger or change the outcome of that crash. I needed, in my mind, to let go and leave whenever I wanted. The memory of retreating onto the balcony was still allowing me to be on recall but gave me breathing space, and a friend for support, in order to do so. The out-of-focus colleagues' opinions or reactions – or lack of them – didn't matter; they hadn't seen what I'd seen or experienced what I'd lived through. My PTSD was an understandable reaction to a massive thing that had happened to me. Suddenly, there seemed to be some clarity. And somehow, that came with relief.

CHAPTER 22
KINTSUGI

That was the worst, and the best, EMDR session to date. It was horrendously distressing; my whole body hurt for the next few days and I seemed to have pulled muscles in my shoulder and upper back, which I attributed to bracing against my "seatbelt". Keith was covering our shift the next day. I had a good catch-up with him first thing that morning, explaining that I was likely to be wobbly as I was still processing from the hardest session I'd experienced so far. But I also described my progress and how the sessions had worked out. I gave him the heads-up, as well, that I'd worried, upset and insulted a few people in the last week, in case anyone approached him! He took it all superbly and was happy to explain to anyone who spoke to him about it, and in fact guide them to me to have any questions answered.

I spent the whole of that shift in a trembling, eye-y,

hypervigilant state. A couple of times, Keith asked me if I needed to go home and book sick as EMDR had been quite intense. Once again, I slept on my lunch break, only to be continually jolted awake by my brain. I managed, somehow, to get to the end of the day – I didn't want to go sick as I knew why I was feeling so off, and that those feelings would ease as my brain worked through what it needed to.

My night shifts were exhausting and I had vet appointments to attend on the days between. This meant I didn't get to catch up on much sleep, which by this time I was desperately craving. My second night shift finished the morning of Christmas Day. I went home, checked on my poorly rabbit, had a nap, and then headed off for Christmas dinner with my family that afternoon. I was still reeling but enjoyed those few hours, before making my excuses and coming away to rest.

Boxing Day saw me wake in a foul, emotional mood as my overwhelm caught up with me. My parents had very kindly invited me round for more food. I felt I couldn't refuse as it was Christmas but I was definitely not in the right headspace to socialise. I arrived, and my exhaustion and emotion turned into anger. I ended up getting cross and stroppy with them, took some food and left them to it. I knew I was in the wrong; I knew I was horrible and ungrateful and rude, but I couldn't explain that I just wanted to be left alone without having to speak to anyone for a couple of days. I desperately needed to withdraw and switch off. My parents rang me repeatedly, worried. I felt bad for making them feel like that; I told them I was fine and I did apologise, but I still couldn't bring myself to be friendly and sociable. I stayed distanced for a couple of days, then went round to visit and tried to be normal. They followed my lead, didn't ask questions and, thankfully, things once again returned to how they had been.

The new year came round: January 2023 was, quite frankly, a revelation. Magic Lady had worked her incredible wizardry during the mammoth EMDR session before Christmas and, after taking several days over the festive period for my brain to process and work through events, things were now inordinately better. Work was amazing. I felt the most calm and in control as I had been in a long, long time; a bit like the old me again. My whole demeanour felt lighter, happier, as though something heavy had lifted from my shoulders and I no longer lived in the depths of despair. My colleagues all noticed it. As the weeks ticked by, I took note of it too, and tried to recognise my new normal. Certain incidents at work still made me a little wobbly or eye-y, but I was able to control it. I still had hypervigilance when driving and with crowds; I still reacted to loud noises. I also noticed I was still using my old coping mechanism of bottling up emotions and stresses so as to deal with what was at hand, but that that quite often overspilled into the next day, leaving me quiet, shaky and more vulnerable. I had emotionally off days, when I felt I couldn't deal with anyone for fear of either shutting down and mentally withdrawing, or losing my cool and insulting them, as I'd done with my family at Christmas. However, I was finding that if I gave myself a day to straighten myself out again, I could then calm that overwhelm. I noticed, too, that stressful experiences would also still come out through nightmares – it seems I do most of my emotional processing at night, so will likely always now be susceptible to this.

My next couple of EMDR sessions saw Magic Lady pleased with the progress we'd made. She believed we had now processed everything there was to process. What was left were residual PTSD symptoms that I would have to learn to manage and control day to day. I was likely always going to be more sensitive to stresses; there was a good chance work would trigger me in the future; I drove a long, fast route on my commute each day, which would always be difficult for me, and the nature of my route automatically increased my chances of stumbling upon, then having to deal with, another collision at some point. But, we were both hopeful that I'd made good enough strides to be able to manage on a daily basis. I needed to learn to recognise when my body was becoming overwhelmed, as my tendency to box stresses up means I don't know what I'm feeling until it explodes into somatic symptoms. This was something I would have to work on constantly; ongoing. I also needed to practise grounding, breathing techniques and coping strategies.

Having reviewed my progress, Magic Lady wanted to space our next session out by a month – giving me some time to adapt, and also allowing for work to throw challenges my way during those four weeks to see how I would cope. In the interim, I decided to make a list of things I had learnt throughout this whole process, with the thought that, perhaps one day, they might aid someone else with their own coping strategies.

First, grounding: I've mentioned this several times

throughout the book. Grounding is meant to be a strategy to bring yourself back to the present moment. It can help if you're feeling panicked, anxious, stressed or overwhelmed. I'll admit, I struggled a lot with this concept. When I'd been deep in a flashback or triggered beyond belief, nothing would work for me; I learnt to just ride it out, stop trying to resist and go with what my body and my mind needed to do to clear it. I struggled to see how I would ever make any grounding techniques work – I wouldn't be thinking straight at the time they were really needed.

However, the trick for me, I've learnt, is to prepare and set things in place beforehand. Being blindsided with a trigger at work is hard to anticipate, but grounding techniques to use for my everyday overwhelm seem to be beneficial. A lot of people use counting games, lists or spotting visual cues around them to bring them back into the moment. I need something tangible; physical. The biggest help for me is fresh air. I will seek the outdoors, regardless of the weather. The change in temperature, the freshness, the wind all alter my senses enough to tether my mind back to the moment. Smells are also a good one. I have a rollerball container of essential oils that was given to me: a strong scent unlike anything else, which shocks me back to reality. Perfume also helps. I nearly always wear a ring on my thumb too. It's designed for people with anxiety and spins like a fidget toy; being multi-coloured and glittery adds to the distraction of it. I play with it when trying to remain in the moment during a particularly challenging situation.

My tattoo is strategically placed as well – on my left forearm, so I can see it both when at work and when in the car.

Secondly, calming techniques: strategies to help me manage day to day, not specifically in trigger moments. Breathing is a big one for me. When stressed, I seem to hold my breath; I can last ages without noticing this, but that then increases the stress coursing around the rest of my body. I'm learning – it's still a work in progress! – to be aware of my breathing and to steady it with deep breaths if needed. Again, I didn't find the counting methods or breathing patterns helpful, but great if they work for you. It makes me feel claustrophobic to count breaths – instead, I just try to fill my lungs with air and exhale deeply until I feel calmer. Usually, if I'm not breathing, my muscles are held tightly clenched. So I'm also trying to remember to relax my body whenever I can.

As well as this, I'm starting to recognise when events might be too overwhelming, and I need to make compromises so I have the experience but can look after my health at the same time. Can I attend an event for a shorter time? Drive and have an easy escape route, if needed? Keep the following day free to regroup and be unsociable so as to settle nerves? Is there going to be somewhere quieter to retreat to if it gets too much? Prepping like this can make all the difference. I've found it helpful to prep others too: if you're putting yourself in a situation you might find difficult, then give those around you a bit of a heads-up; tell them how they can help if you start to struggle.

Find something that calms you; something you enjoy doing – and make sure you interject some of that self-care into your week. For me, the odd outdoor swim, or just an afternoon with my bunnies, helps me regroup. Animals are powerful healers.

Thirdly, here are a few lessons I've picked up on my PTSD journey. It's been helpful to me to finally grasp them, so having them to refer to here might help others too:

- It's ok to lean on people; actually, it's sometimes necessary to do so. Throughout my life, I have always been proudly, fiercely independent. That was fine – until I became unwell. I've learnt I can't rely on my own strength and resilience if that's what has been shaken by illness. Trust loved ones around you; allow them to support you the way you would support them, and they will help you pull yourself through to the other side. People genuinely want to help.

- Be honest. If somebody asks if you're ok, tell them the truth. If you mask it, they can't help you. If you insist you're fine, they'll stop checking in because they believe you, or they'll assume you don't need help. Be brutally, totally honest: if you're struggling, say so. If you need to talk or want company, shout. Only then can things be done. There's no bravery in putting on a brave face.

- Be scared – but do it anyway. I have only made progress and gained momentum by pushing forwards. Even when I didn't want to; even when it was terrifying. Even when all I wanted to do was curl up in bed and ignore the world. Get up, face it, be scared – but triumph over it. Grit is a powerful quality to have.

- Ask for and accept all the help that is offered to you. I've completed two types of therapy; I've visited the Fire Fighters Charity twice. I had to reach out and ask for those opportunities, apply and be assessed. Without having done that, I'm pretty sure I wouldn't still be here. But no one else could do those things for me: it was up to me to help myself.

- Have hope. Try to remember, when in the depths of despair, that things have a way of working out.

- There is no timeframe on recovery. I witnessed my initial trauma in August 2016. PTSD raised its head in August 2021. Today, in 2023, I'm still healing. I've learnt to listen to my own body, my own mind, and to go at my own pace. Don't let outside influences dictate to you where you "should" be – and be patient with yourself.

- Talk. Everybody is going through something. I've found that, by talking about my own situation, it's helped others to open up about their lives too. Sometimes there have been things we could each relate to and help each other with. And if there weren't, then the conversation would serve as an explanation as to what I'd been experiencing and why I might have been behaving as I was.

- Be grateful. For life. For the loved ones in your life willing to stick by your side. For the small things.

- You must come first. If someone's connection to you costs more than it brings value or positivity, then perhaps re-evaluate that relationship. If a situation sends you into a spin unnecessarily, then withdraw. Your health and wellbeing must be a priority – more so than trying to please the world around you.

- On a practical note, my final point is that I always now have my mobile phone within reach when I'm in the car. It will be held in the cradle on the dashboard or stored in my jacket pocket, and connected to hands-free where possible. I will never again put myself in a position where something happens and I'm unable even to ring for help. Equally, though, I stringently follow the law in regard to touching my phone when driving. Emergencies are one thing, but I've seen what happens when a person flouts the rules and becomes distracted in their vehicle. I would never forgive myself if I caused that level of devastation for the sake of something inconsequential.

Following all this – what I've been through, what I've learnt – I've been on a bit of a mission. I've continued to write this book, with the intention that it might offer hope or a kind of kinship to those struggling with trauma. I would love to see it become something that perhaps the Fire Fighters Charity can refer people to, or talk to other control rooms about. At the time of writing this, I have a meeting scheduled with Keith and the wellbeing manager of the brigade, in the hope of implementing some ideas to improve the service's approach to trauma and to PTSD.

My personal life has certainly changed too. I've had to adapt to what I'm comfortable doing socially, which is a massive thing for someone who would previously book a plane flight at the drop of a hat and go on adventures. My relationships with friends and family have altered too. My civilian friends in particular have struggled to understand the challenges I've had to face and, to be fair, I've found them more difficult to engage with as well. I no longer speak to Georgia; sadly, after many years of friendship, we reached the end of the road for us. I've experienced something similar with a couple of other friendships, where I believe my mental illness caused too much stress for them to deal with. However, other connections have strengthened on the back of this process: Beth, Lucy and Sasha have all been their amazing, lovely selves, and have always been there whenever I've wanted to meet up or chat.

My work friends, too, have been phenomenal; I am so, so lucky to have had such fantastic support. Daniel, Richard, Clara and Jon especially have all been fabulous, picking me up so many times when I've been terrified or distraught, and always being at the end of the phone to let me vent. Marcus, Lily, Harriet, Amy and the rest of Blue Watch deserve a special mention – I couldn't have asked for anyone better to be with me along my journey. They've been supportive and non-judgemental; allowed me to react however I needed to; and were also brave enough to speak up when they were struggling to deal with me themselves. I am so grateful for that. At the time, as I've described, I felt like a complete burden to them. In retrospect, I can see they were actively avoiding my becoming so; trying to help themselves while still helping me.

Management, including Keith, Sam and Debbie, have offered the guidance and support I have desperately needed throughout this whole process. Despite a few blips along the way, where perhaps my emotional state left me less tolerant with them, I owe my return to work and my own sanity largely to their patience, acceptance and belief that there was an end in sight.

My family have borne the brunt of my mood swings and have probably been left out of the loop the most throughout this. I am so sorry to have hurt or offended them; not at all my intention. A lot of my silence was me trying to deal with what was being thrown at me. As I improve, I hope to open up more with them; it'll be nice to be able to tell them everything, but in the past tense, when there is no longer any danger of stressing or worrying them.

I am now at a point where I consider myself once again competent in my job role as a fire control operator. I'm able to live my life, socialise, and deal with what life throws at me. I just have to be prepared that it won't always be as easy for me to cope as other people find it, and indeed that I won't always be able to deal with things the way I have in the past. I believe I will always be a little bit broken, but if I can continue to live – not just survive – and help others while I do so, then I'm ok with that. I'm a little proud too. It would have been so easy on so many occasions to just give up: therapy, my job, friends, everything. I'm so glad my stubborn streak persisted and I worked to meet every challenge head on.

I will always refer to myself as "broken" – half-jokingly, but with no negative connotations. That turn of phrase makes me think back to my late teenage years when, in my first ever job working in retail, we used to sell versions of a specific type of Japanese pottery: a style known as Kintsugi. This was usually crockery that was broken, but had been put back together using lacquer infused with gold. The idea is that breakages are to be celebrated; flaws should be embraced. And, despite the fact that sometimes things shatter, one should remain hopeful: they can become whole again; scarred but better and now more valuable. These fragile items are transformed into something stronger than ever before.

I now consider my mental health as a human form of Kintsugi. I think of myself as broken but rebuilt; resilient, and having learnt lessons and gained experience along the way that have produced the gold with which I've managed to glue all my shattered pieces back together.

Printed in Great Britain
by Amazon